A Great Place to Learn & Earn

Also by David J. Waldron:

Build Wealth With Common Stocks

Hire Train Monitor Motivate

The Ten Domains of Effective Goal Setting

A Great Place to Learn & Earn

An Organizational Effectiveness Model for Career Sector Education's Critical Role in Twenty-First Century Workforce Development

David J. Waldron

Country View

Country View
https:/davidjwaldron.com
Carlisle, Pennsylvania, USA

First Edition
Printed by Kindle Direct Publishing, an Amazon.com company.
21 16 15   3 1 2 3 11

ISBN-13: 978-0692511701 / ISBN-10: 0692511709

Original and modified cover art by NaCDS and Cover Design Studio
Cover image by Trevor Lush from Dianne Falk, Cardinal Marketing
Interior Design created with IngramSpark Book Building Tool
Publishing imprint by Birendra at Logo Design Team
Author profile photo by Gene Hutnak Photography

For Suzan, thank you for the unconditional love, steadfast support, and fabulous instincts. You are my inspiration.

CONTENTS

A Great Place to Learn & Earn is the culmination of more than two decades of learning and practicing in the for-profit postsecondary career education sector as an admissions representative, director of admissions, and campus president. I began formalizing the principles around 2005 and used it as a template for an on-ground career school that we built from about three hundred and fifty students to over one thousand in five years. Despite this rapid growth, the campus enjoyed a strong compliance record, including zero findings of noncompliance on both an institutional accreditation renewal visit and on-site federal program review.

During this time frame, I was given an opportunity to present the concepts of *A Great Place to Learn & Earn* at a companywide meeting of campus presidents. Several years later, one attendee at the original meeting was awarded school leader of the year. As I was congratulating her, she offered that my presentation was an inspiration for her performance and had applied the principles of *A Great Place to Learn & Earn* during her campus's rise to award-winning status. I was humbled as much as honored. From that moment, I was inspired to share these concepts with interested professionals affiliated with the sector whose performance or perceptions might benefit as a result.

My goal is to present *A Great Place to Learn & Earn* as a catalyst, a blueprint of organizational, team, and individual effectiveness in the postsecondary career education sector. My professional memoir as a proud and successful veteran of this vital sector where aspiring students, and other motivated stakeholders, learn and earn from the benefits of career-focused education.

Of late, this learn and earn edict is being threatened by the gainful employment regulations from the U.S. Department of Education, targeted at for-profit institutions. When was the last time you met a traditional college student, perhaps yourself included, who denied the primary motivation for their enrollment was career attainment via gainful employment? Nonetheless, I submit the career education sector's best days are ahead. In the interim, a continued shakeout may be necessary to rid the few bad apples that have brought unwanted attention and additional oversight, any inherent profit motive prejudice from opponents notwithstanding.

In this spirit, the nine chapters of *A Great Place to Learn & Earn* strive to offer a simple yet inspiring template for career education sector companies and institutions that are seeking to achieve or sustain a high quality and profitable organization by focusing on what is necessary to the success of students, employers, and other principal stakeholders.

Making a Living, Making a Difference is a brief autobiography of my multi-year tenure in the career education sector. I believe it is essential to share my journey by presenting each chapter with clarity and genuine intent. People Before Vision presents a classic paradox in organizational effectiveness, first conveyed by author Jim Collins in his classic, *Good to Great*. Collins's book was the primary inspiration during my leadership of several award-winning campuses.

Campus of Distinction examines strategies to nurture an on-ground operation, online platform, or company toward excellence in a student-centric environment. Hire Train Monitor Motivate assesses how to generate institutional quality from an employee-driven culture. Playing the Game the Right Way provides an operational model with a history of delivering outstanding student and institutional outcomes.

Stakeholder Driven Decision Making speaks to balancing the demands of seven interested participants by first adopting a leadership model of inclusion and then driving an economic model of mutually dependent engines. Hello Zones and More Simple Rules for Everyday Success identifies a commitment paradigm to career achievement, and not just for students. This chapter includes practical rules to implement on campus, online, or corporate, plus how to confront the challenging aspects of being a role model in career education today.

Navigating the Higher Education Industrial Complex is a compilation of my public comments in a less than humble defense of the career education sector and its ethical stakeholders. It attempts to explore how to operate and compete in the throes of the ever-present higher education industrial complex comprised of traditional and nontraditional postsecondary education, the mainstream media, policy think tanks, and a divided political landscape.

A Great Place to Learn & Earn concludes with A Renewed Value Proposition for Postsecondary Career Education in anticipation of the sector's stakeholders redefining critical roles necessary to remain active participants in twenty-first century workforce development.

Hundreds of mentors, peers, and protégés influenced my rewarding tenure in career education; partners of distinction to whom I owe my sincerest gratitude for impressing on my performance, and most importantly, for the positive outcomes of thousands of student customers.

To each influential partner; to the millions of students whose lives are improving through career education; to the passionate, caring faculty and staff that teach and support the students; and to all readers, whether active stakeholders or interested observers, I thank you for your tireless contributions to our sector's noble and worthy mission.

Sincerely,

David J. Waldron

August 24, 2015

One

MAKING A LIVING, MAKING A DIFFERENCE

WE MAKE A LIVING BY WHAT WE GET. WE
MAKE A LIFE BY WHAT WE GIVE.
—SIR WINSTON CHURCHILL

In the career education sector—unlike most other businesses and organizations—after selling the product or service to your customer, i.e., enroll a student, you spend significant time throughout the next one to four years, or more, with that customer in the same building or online forum.

During job conversations with family and friends, discussions about customers and clients presume each is at arm's length via email, phone, webinar, plane, train, automobile, or a brief visit to a retail establishment. On the contrary, at a career sector school, college, or university, an entire workday can be in the presence of your student customer, albeit in the classroom, office, hallway, or online platform. It is an emotional and physical drain, countered by an exhilarating feeling of doing a job with a calling far above its monetary reward of a paycheck and benefits package. You are making a living, making a difference.

And yes, the career education sector company that employs you is making a profit by making a difference. But the common denominator is making a difference in the lives of students that have entrusted valuable time, tuition dollars, and dreams of a better life for themselves and their loved ones. Whether a private investor or shareholder; corporate executive or staffer; campus administrator, faculty or staff; vendor or employer; accreditor or regulator; you go to work, in large part, to provide a better life for you and your family. To offer anything less to your students is duplicitous and insincere. The students deserve as much, and as a stakeholder in the public interest, you are accountable to each one.

These are challenging times in career education. Federal and state regulators, traditional higher education, and the mainstream media have painted the sector as a singular bad actor. But it is a sector of passionate, ethical difference-makers sidestepped by a few bad players that deserve no place in this valued profession of career-focused education. The potential exists to serve the fifty-eight percent of adult Americans with a high school diploma or equivalent, although less than a college degree. Higher education providers in the sector enjoy the potential to serve adult Americans pursuing bachelors and advanced degrees by way of convenient student-centered platforms.

You may know who the bad actors are, in the minority nonetheless, although it is in your best interest to wish each one away—by whistleblowing, if appropriate—before the government does. Bad actors prevail in every industry. But analogous to the squares of Medieval Europe, in a public interest field such as postsecondary education, each stands out as an alleged criminal awaiting their fate at the hands of everyday citizens. The career education sector's recent attempt to solve its problems by voting on party lines was not the answer. Playing the game the right way was, and remains, the appropriate response.

I believe in career education. Always have and will. My late, enlightened father said, "For-profit or nonprofit, remember it is about the money." Whether for-profit or nonprofit, successful organizations in our society are deemed prosperous by generating surplus dollars from favorable customer experiences. The organization's tax status determines whether any surplus is shared internally as a nonprofit or universally as a for-profit. In either case, the community wins.

Of course, it is not fruitful when organizations lose money because of eroding customer confidence. Profit or nonprofit, the organization, its stakeholders, and the surrounding community each pay a price for operational or financial failure.

But in the current regulatory climate, including the struggles with high tuition and corresponding student loan debt— issues hampering traditional education as well—it is incumbent upon stakeholders in the career education sector to unite behind a sustainable mission:

An ethical, high-quality, student-centered, outcomes-driven, affordable education for the benefit of our fellow citizens seeking a better life through gainful employment from career-focused education and training.

A Journey of Professional Self Discovery

My story of entering the postsecondary career education space dates back to the 1980s. As a recent college graduate at the time, I worked in a progression of career fields seeking to find my professional way. The experience was reminiscent of Billy Crystal's character in the comedy, *City Slickers* (Culver City, CA: Columbia Pictures, 1991), who laments, "My twenties were a blur."

As a young adult, I yearned for a career to make a good living and make a difference in people's lives. In that spirit, I first applied to my undergraduate college as an environmental science major.

During campus visitation day, this naïve eighteen-year-old high school senior attended the faculty-sponsored environmental studies workshop, finding to my surprise, the projected job opportunities included testing water samples from offshore oil rigs. I remember thinking to myself: *If I am going to work for Exxon, I might as well spend my days in the comforts of an office building with perhaps a better paycheck.* I changed my major to business studies on that day. It is conceivable my sudden transformation was driven by an economic vulnerability, although I have no regrets.

Following graduation from college, I ventured through my blurry twenties, longing for that elusive career juxtaposition of earning well by helping well. My newly minted business mind evaluated the apparent opportunities. Social worker? Noble, but low-paying. Selling widgets? Good pay, yet little value proposition. Physician? The ultimate well-paid difference maker, although I was not getting into medical school anytime soon. Lawyer? The well-intended dream for my vocation by my late, wonderful mother, who retired as the executive assistant to a community college president. But as said in the sarcasm laced New York metropolitan area where I grew up, "Forget about it." My search for the perfect career continued unabated.

As a business professional wannabe with a mandatory subscription to *Fortune* magazine, I ran across a fascinating article in the mid-1980s on economic prognostications for the late twentieth and early twenty-first centuries. Predicting the future is problematic in general, although a fool's game in economics and finance. But for a career desperate, soul-searching young adult, required reading nonetheless.

What captured my attention was a section in the article committed to adult training, or how career-focused education was moving beyond the post-high school traditional college model by providing opportunities for students older than the typical eighteen to twenty-four-year-old age group. The late John Sperling's start-up, the University of Phoenix, and its degree completion education platform for working adults were presented as metaphors. The difference-maker was Phoenix, and similar institutions were expanding beyond traditional colleges' limitations and making a profit doing so.

The proverbial palm landed on my premature receding hairline. I could make a good living and make a difference by offering career training opportunities for motivated adults. The article shared that just one in four adult Americans had earned at least a bachelor's degree. The college-educated at the time more often came from privileged backgrounds. These folks were lucky to pull the long straw at birth, as legendary investor Warren Buffett reminds us. What were the other seventy-five percent supposed to do? Feel sorry to be unlucky in pulling the short straw, or do something about their fate? Each one deserved a chance at the American Dream as much as anyone, I thought. And if the *Fortune* article was correct, students might seek this adult training paradigm in droves.

Seven years after receiving my bachelor's degree in business—by way of an indirect environmental sciences pathway—I had decided on a career choice with an opportunity to make a living, making a difference.

No friend or family member called to steer me to this vital industry that I refer to in the book as the postsecondary career education sector. I had no connections that I was aware of, although six degrees of separation led to my first job in the field. What it did necessitate was the desire to make a living by making a difference, coupled with a coincidental subscription to the top business publication for the time. Nevertheless, it was three years before I attained my newfound professional dream come true.

The Impetus of Turning Thirty and Getting Married

By 1991, I was in my early thirties and engaged to my wife, Suzan, events that hastened my goal of making a living by making a difference. If there were ever two moments to kick oneself into gear, becoming thirty-something and greeting the love of your life at the altar, were the ultimate self-motivators.

One Sunday, a pre-internet advertisement jumped off the help wanted classified pages of the *Newark Star-Ledger* seeking an admissions representative for Katharine Gibbs School in Montclair, New Jersey. When I called the director of admissions at the number listed, to my surprise, it was a gentleman who once worked in the same office building at the Jersey Shore as I did. He sold advertising for the local newspaper, and I peddled top forty bands to hotel cocktail lounges nationwide for an entertainment company. The talent office was the hip place to gravitate and he visited often, expressing an unrelenting sense of humor and excellent sales skills. I welcomed his comedic timing and loved to talk sales technique with him. As fate later dictated, he offered me the job at Gibbs.

But it was more than just about whom you know. Prospective admissions representatives at Gibbs had to pass a sales acuity test administered, via telephone, by the Gallop Organization. My scheduled interview ended in ten minutes. Excited, I called my supposed future director of admissions to tell him I had completed the test within minutes. He uttered, "Oops, that means you did not pass the screener." In other words, I had failed the assessment that determines whether one is qualified to take the test in the first place.

My dream of making a living and making a difference in the career education sector had reached a potentially fatal stumbling block. As fate had it again, during the interview process, I was fortunate to have impressed the campus president as well, and they found a way to hire me with immunity.

As it went, the advertising salesperson that converted to a director of admissions became a great trainer and mentor for the entertainment salesperson hoping to become an admissions high achiever. But that was before a torrid first ninety days where I was unable to persuade more than a few students to enroll, despite a fair amount of interviews showing at the door from my telephone work.

I sat with the director of admissions and went through each documented student interview dissecting my performance of good, bad, and ugly. Besides reminding me about technique, he discussed the importance of centering on the prospective student and presuming when one shows up at the door, the message conveyed is, "I want to do this." You then either show the prospective student the way or sabotage their commitment. I learned how to get out of my way and that of the student; to be a mentor and pathway instead of just another obstacle builder in their life. The job became fun.

Despite the poor test result, suggesting probable failure at career college admissions, I went on to what was known as high achiever status in my first full year by starting one hundred and sixty-five new students. But as a self-proclaimed difference-maker, enrolling new students was just the beginning of my commitment. In a notebook and the hallway, I tracked each of my students. About seventy-six percent graduated, often to dream jobs or promotions.

I will forever remember a letter from a once difficult prospective student that I had interviewed several times over two years before starting school and completing her program. In her correspondence, she boasted about the job she secured at the headquarters of brokerage Merrill Lynch and had earned several promotions since. She thanked me as a mentor for helping end her lack of follow-through and self-sabotage, providing motivation to fulfill her dream of completing an education and starting a career. I read the letter with happy tears, knowing I had done nothing other than showing her the way, and to her credit, she followed through with great success.

After overcoming the doldrums-filled first ninety days, I remember sharing with Suzan that I had found my calling and planned to make postsecondary career education a permanent endeavor. My objective was to become the director of admissions, then a campus president, within seven years.

I achieved the goal in six years and ten months when after a successful stint as director of admissions at Gibbs College in Norwalk, Connecticut, I was named campus president of the original Katharine Gibbs

School in Providence, Rhode Island. The Ocean State became our new home and permanent residence.

After tripling the Providence student population with positive outcomes and strong regulatory compliance, obtaining degree-granting approval from the state legislature—the first for-profit to do so in Rhode Island history—and planning a new sixty thousand square foot campus, I went on to other valuable and memorable campus leadership roles. Gibbs College of Boston was followed by a brief stint at Kaplan Higher Education, also in the Boston metro. I was then recruited back to Rhode Island by Lincoln Educational Services, where I enjoyed my career's longest tenure.

I have since retired from day-to-day campus operations to write and offer advisory services on organizational effectiveness in postsecondary career education as a way to give back to the sector that defined me as a professional.

Thanks to the career education sector and the opportunities it affords students—in partnership with the stakeholders that teach and support each one—I was now making a living, making a difference.

Two

PEOPLE BEFORE VISION

GREAT VISION WITHOUT GREAT PEOPLE IS
IRRELEVANT. —JIM COLLINS

In his seminal book, *Good to Great* (Harper Business),[1] Jim Collins and his research team studied organizations that transformed from mere good companies to great, legendary enterprises. The team found several common denominators in the companies studied, and many of the shared traits were paradoxical or countered to conventional wisdom.

Whereas business books are the proverbial dime a dozen, *Good* to *Great* is considered among the best written. I am in that camp and have chosen its key concepts as the foundation of this chapter to demonstrate how career education schools and companies can make what Collins described as "the leap to greatness."

* * *

[1] *GOOD TO GREAT – Why Some Companies Make the Leap...and Others Don't.* Copyright © 2001 by Jim Collins. Published by Harper Business (an imprint of HarperCollins Publishers, Inc.) For more information, visit www.jimcollins.com. Reprinted with permission of Curtis Brown, Ltd.

People First, Then Culture

His initial concept is perhaps the most paradoxical of Collins's conclusions. He discovered that the great companies first hired the best talent each could find and afford and then allowed those people to determine the organization's vision and mission. In other words, let the capable people hired create the culture of the company. Collins translated his notion into a believable concept by asking, "First who, then what?"

He envisioned a successful organization driving a bus down a highway unaware of where it was journeying, although to a presumed place of greatness. According to Collins, the great companies:

- First, get the right people on the bus.
- Then, get the wrong people off the bus.
- Next, put the right people in the right seats.
- And then, let the right people in the right seats figure out where to drive the bus.

It is rare to find such a compelling paradigm in today's workplace, the career education sector being no exception, in general. Often the vision is set at the top; then, talent is sought to fit into that vision's culture. But does it work?

To test the typical vision first, people second culture found in most organizations today, ask a well-regarded employee or coworker what they think of your organization's vision and culture. Political correctness notwithstanding, you can expect a positive, albeit brief, and to the point answer. Then ask what they prefer to add or delete from the published vision, mission, and values statements. I guarantee the time spent answering your follow-up question will far exceed the first. The concept of people first is manifested because motivated employees prefer to be a harbinger of the vision instead of a mere follower.

So how do you find outstanding, self-disciplined employees and coworkers?

Interview for Greatness

Hire or refer disciplined people. I have long observed the second you need to micromanage someone, you have made a hiring mistake. But Collins asks, "What if we manage systems, not people?"

He found this approach superior because you evade hierarchy, bureaucracy, or excessive controls when you have disciplined people, thought, and action. In the great companies that Collins researched, these hiring practices came before any deep analysis of required credentials or practical skills.

To demonstrate a real-world example of putting discipline, talent, and commitment ahead of credentials, I once ran a career college where I had stopped counting how many students had expressed that a particular faculty member was the best teacher ever since kindergarten. This coveted instructor was a disciplinarian who maintained classroom control, although she taught in a kind, dedicated, and thoughtful manner. And students respected her consistency. She was a born teacher, yet never took her natural talent for granted, working hard and going above and beyond for her students without letting any off the hook. In the eyes of students, peers, and administrators, she was the best.

Nevertheless, while pursuing regional accreditation to replace our national accreditation, and although the instructor had a bachelor's degree from an Ivy League university in the subject matter taught, the accreditation visiting team determined she was no longer eligible to teach specific courses. Her master's degree was not in the field as required by the standards. Best teacher ever, but lacked the proper credential. I wanted to give a copy of *Good to Great* to each member of the accreditation team.

It was no surprise this same great instructor displayed four personality traits that I found as a hiring manager often predicted employees' success in career training environments.

Four Traits of a Successful Career Education Employee:

- Assertive - a values-driven communicator.
- Self-directed - performs with limited or no supervision.
- Other-directed - demonstrates genuine customer focus.
- Work ethic - exhibits dedication and character.

Two immutable keys to the four traits of a successful career education professional are 1) the employee must own all four with some significance, and 2) you must discover the qualities in the hiring process because they cannot be taught.

Assertive does not mean aggressive. Ethical, confident professionals demonstrate a substantial capacity for communicating well with a focus on values and problem-solving. During the formal interview, ask the candidate to share how they identified and solved a pressing problem in the workplace. The answer will demonstrate professional assertiveness or lack thereof.

Next, take the prospective employee on a tour of the campus or office building, using it as an opportunity to observe interactions with faculty, staff, and students. Thriving education and training operations, particularly those with challenging student populations, require employees with ethical assertiveness.

Self-directed, also expressed as self-motivated, characterizes the discipline of the employee when left with limited supervision. But do not ask the candidate direct questions about self-motivation as good interviewees—not necessarily good employees— will have prepared answers they assume you want to hear. Instead, challenge the candidate with questions about specific projects or job duties they were forced to complete independently. Listen to how confident they were in tackling and completing tasks at work, including unpopular ones.

Other-directed, often described as customer service, has become a dinosaur in commerce today. But avoid confusing this trait with outgoing, friendly personalities as most people in society, and therefore, workplaces, are extroverted. It is best to have caring and motivated professionals—including introverts—who are genuine about taking care of the customer, whether student, employer, coworker, accreditor, or regulator.

During the hiring process, ask the candidate their perception of the roles of teaching or serving students and other stakeholders. The answer should equate to: "I love doing this so much; getting paid a fair wage for it is a bonus!"

Work ethic is perhaps the one trait most associated with the expression, "You cannot teach that." But it involves more than just showing up on time, putting in the necessary effort to get the job done, or being responsible for the workload. Work ethic is more about character and self-discipline.

Taking responsibility, avoiding impulsive behavior, and taking the high road, are common in those with a sound work ethic. Interview questions are simple: "Bring me through a typical workday from arrival to departure. Tell me about the last time you were in an unexpected confrontation with a customer or coworker. How did you handle it?" Get to the character of the candidate.

Assertive, self-motivated, customer-centered employees who demonstrate a strong work ethic and self-discipline will often prevail in the career education sector's performance-driven cultures.

Lead or Follow with Professional Will and Personal Humility

Whether you approach work as a leader or a follower—granted successful teams need both—Collins discovered the great organizations exhibited uncommon workplace habits where each:

- Focus on what to do, what not to do, and what to stop doing.
- Take credit for bad performance and give credit for good performance.
- Lead by asking questions, more so than providing answers.
- Engage in dialogue and debate, not coercion.
- Conduct necessary autopsies fixated on solutions, not blame.

Imagine a corporate or campus culture that allows the questioning of processes; takes responsibility when things do not go as well as planned; is devoid of having every answer, yet engages with questioning to empower as opposed to stymie; facilitates open dialogue in problem-solving; and investigates issues for resolution instead of culpability. What if there were no written warnings, no annual performance reviews, no Bible-long rules of conduct, no wrenching restructuring, cost-cutting, or other repressive tactics that paralyze more than stimulate an organization?

What if department managers ran companies or campuses instead of well-intentioned, although sometimes destructive, legal and human resource departments? Collins's great companies were magnificent because each first hired and nurtured disciplined people, then let those people drive the bus to greatness.

Confront the Brutal Facts and Do the Right Thing

Collins also found that companies making the leap from good to great had a consistent belief in the ability to succeed in the end. He contends, "If a company conducts due diligence and gathers the facts, the right path will often unfold right in front of it."

His terrific analogy is of a large flywheel that takes relentless pushing to turn just once. However, after spinning in the same direction over time, it starts to gain momentum until it becomes a dominant force on its own. Collins suggests that good to great transformation does not happen overnight but results from years of persistence. It might look dramatic and revolutionary from the outside; however, on the inside, it is more an organic development process.

In the current climate of regulatory pressure, negative media coverage, and dwindling enrollment in the career education sector, a willingness first to confront the brutality it faces and then make the appropriate corrections has become the sector's heart and soul's quest for survival.

Drive Your Economic Engine

> Adequate new enrollment + quality education + ethical graduation rate + high job placement = a profitable career education enterprise.

In Collins's book, the good to great companies branded and drove economic engines, the ultimate achievement for being in existence as a business in the first place. During my three decades in the workplace, it became apparent how people and organizations get sidetracked from the economic mission, often the company's founding purpose.

For the career education sector, driving its economic engine is as simple as adequate new enrollment, plus quality education, plus ethical graduation rates, plus high job placement, equal a profitable enterprise.

But this formula for success has no room for predatory recruiting, devalued instructional costs, grade inflation, or minimal job placement standards. On the contrary, it takes a disciplined and caring environment focused on doing the right thing by hiring and retaining employees that recruit, train, support, and job place qualified students to each stakeholder's advantage. Constituents that benefit include students, employers, accreditors, regulators, shareholders, and the public at large.

Understanding and driving your campus or company's economic engine is a fundamental requirement of a successful organization. Ignore or compromise your engine, and it will seize.

What Can Your Campus Be the Best in the World At?

A central theme for the great companies in Collins's research was, "What can your organization be the best in the world at?" Successful companies want to know the one big audacious thing they can understand and commit. What does the institution employ as its core solution to competitive threats and changes in the industry? Think gainful employment. What must you be passionate about, best in the world, and make a profit or surplus by doing so?

I challenge readers, regardless of whether affiliated with a campus, regional division, corporate office, regulatory agency, accrediting body, employer, investor, or work outside of the career education sector, to engage your colleagues by asking the question, "What can we be the best in the world at?" You might be amazed at the passionate contributions to this exercise.

For example, at a career school that I led as executive director, we made an effort to hire the best talent available and often asked the question, "What are or can we be the best and most passionate in the world at?" The consensus was campus event management, evidenced by robust and willing participation throughout the faculty, staff, and administration ranks. The improvements in student enrollment, retention, and placement, capped by a spectacular graduation ceremony from this joint effort in event planning and execution, were significant. We became known as the company's preeminent campus for event management and were asked to share our best practices with other locations nationwide.

People Before Vision puts great teams on the career education sector bus, who drive it on a successful journey determined to benefit interested stakeholders. An emphasis is placed on the journey, as opposed to the destination, as a voyage of greatness will endure far beyond any finite endpoint.

In the spirit of Jim Collins's *Good to Great*, you and your educational organization deserve to be on a journey of greatness. Be committed first to hiring and retaining the best people possible, i.e., employees that are assertive, self-directed, customer-focused, and possess a strong work ethic. Show up every day with a professional will tempered by personal humility. Be willing to confront reality, and do the right thing. Drive a culture of discipline in a caring way. Remain forever focused on your economic engine. Work tirelessly to turn your organization's flywheel until it spins in perpetuity. First, identify what you and your coworkers do well, and then be the best in the world at it.

Three

CAMPUS OF DISTINCTION

QUALITY IS NOT AN ACT. IT IS A HABIT.
—ARISTOTLE

What often lies at the heart of dissension between traditional higher education and for-profit career education is the latter's commitment to putting the student at the center of its universe. The former operates under the premise of faculty-centric shared governance, placing the student as an invited guest, albeit a paying one.

Pundits sometimes argue that for-profit education puts the investor first. This reasoning has its merits in the legal presumption that publicly held companies must place shareholders' interests above all else. But in the context of working at the campus level, ground or online, assume the shareholders are taken care of by the corporate office, and your attention is where it needs to be: on the student's well-being as a paying customer.

It is essential to operate a student-centric, career education campus without compromising the needs of other stakeholders such as owners, management, faculty, staff, employers, vendors, and regulators. A consensus-driven culture of teamwork, performance, compliance, and recognition—centered on successful student outcomes—forms the foundation for a company or campus of distinction.

Teamwork: Getting Along

Building consensus begins with collaboration. As discussed in Chapter Two: People Before Vision, hire the best talent available, then allow that talent to drive the bus to greatness per Jim Collins's *Good to Great* paradox. Incorporate definitive ways of developing teams driven by accord; groups that enjoy working together to be the best in the world at what its members are passionate about.

I have observed the most productive teams are the ones that debate or argue over policies, ideas, or student welfare. It is because everyone involved cares. Compassion is an essential ingredient for building and sustaining success in a career education environment.

Consensus building is most challenging between self-interested departments, sometimes labeled as silos. Well-managed career sector schools, colleges, and universities break down silos by encouraging cooperation among department leaders, often spreading throughout the ranks.

Facilitating regular communication between departments is another key to building consensus. Unless already doing so, contribute in your accepted ways to make engagements motivating, productive, and measurable.

Staff meetings play a significant role in team building. Faculty inservice between academic terms are crucial for meeting accreditation standards and are excellent catalysts for building consensus among instructional staff, including on a cross-program basis.

As a rule, consensus-building starts at the top with the campus president or director in partnership with department leaders. Management teams that promote openness, constructive feedback, visibility, and trust, will build a one college team united for the betterment of its students and the employers that hire successful graduates.

Performance: Getting It Done

I have never worked in a more performance-driven culture than found on career education campuses. Excellent student outcomes, consistent employer satisfaction, strong regulatory compliance, profitable share-holder returns, and workplace fulfilled faculty and staff are the order of any sustainable postsecondary career education institution. Helping people and making the numbers must coexist for a campus or company to be successful.

Depending on the employee's personality: people-focused or num-bers-driven, heads spin from the sheer volume of responsibilities. It is a work environment requiring an individual or team's ability to keep sev-eral balls in the air at once. To illustrate, travel a typical student timeline in the career education sector:

> Student enrolls → completes financial aid package → attends orientation → endures the add/drop period → survives to the end of each term → gets to the business office with tuition payments → consults education and financial aid departments to main-tain satisfactory academic progress → all the while engaged in classrooms, labs, tutoring and study groups → visits career ser-vices for resume review and a mock interview → completes any required externships, internships, or certifications → attends job fairs and employer interviews → begins new career → marches in graduation ceremony → pays down student loans on time → refers new students to alma mater.

Amid this integral student activity, the campus and company are committed to a parallel focus on institutional and programmatic ac-creditation standards; state regulations; Title IV administrative capabil-ity; employee recruitment and training; human resource policy; facilities management; information technology infrastructure; campus safety and security; legal disputes; corporate reporting requirements; student services; and the ever expected, although precisely unexpected, interruption or surprise.

In other words, you just remembered the need to conduct an emergency drill as the quarter is nearing an end. And the company has informed you a member of Congress is scheduled to visit the campus on Tuesday. It is never-ending.

A postsecondary career education operation is a haven of people and numbers, driven by outcomes. It is not for the faint of heart. It takes a capacity for empathy, resilience, and emotional intelligence to navigate and survive an atmosphere fixated on performance.

When the going gets tough, do what you do best. Enroll a student, package a student, or tutor a student, bring a student to make a tuition payment, or place a student in an externship, internship, or permanent job. And if drained of emotion, as a result, attend a graduation ceremony. It is the cure for what ails you at a career school, college, or university.

Although, upon returning to the campus or office, you will be reminded that efforts are not confused with performance. It is about getting it done and done right.

Compliance: Getting It Right

In recent years, growing numbers of sector participants have placed a renewed emphasis on regulatory compliance. What is perplexing are ethics, adherence to regulations, and playing the game right have always been paramount to survival in the career education sector. The compelling reason for the enduring and ever-increasing regulatory oversight is companies are making a profit from a service held as a socialistic endeavor within our capitalistic society.

The sector might forever operate with its back to the wall. It remains the target of a vast and growing constituency that finds it tolerable for a public university football coach to be paid millions of dollars a year coaching about one hundred student-athletes, although unacceptable for an investor to profit from capitalizing a company or campus to the direct benefit of thousands of students.

I often spar with the anti-profit education crowd in the comment section of a national publication devoted to higher education. My argument is you can justify generating a profit by making a difference in students' lives, many of whom are ironic casualties of the traditional nonprofit education sector. But conventional wisdom remains that ethical learning outcomes are the exclusive domain of state-owned public or private nonprofit colleges and universities.

Where I lose the naysayers is the general belief in the nonprofit sector that it is appropriate for individual professors to earn six-figure salaries, athletic coaches seven figures, and endowment investment managers more, but intolerable for organizations to profit at any level. A for-profit enterprise is an association of individuals as well. And the corporation pays real and personal property and income taxes in addition to the customary payroll taxes, thereby providing a tangible financial return to the community.

Tax contributions aside, it is an accusation of "shame on you" for making a profit from education. As a campus president in the sector, I was presenting to a state regulatory body that oversaw proprietary schools as well as the state-owned colleges and one university. A board member challenged me on why I needed to make a profit from educating students. My impromptu answer was, "Why is it okay for the state university basketball coach to be paid eight times the salary I receive as a career college president?" Her muddled response: "I am against profiting from education. No more questions."

Regardless, it is inexcusable for a for-profit education company to have the phrase "be ethical" listed as the eleventh commandment of a top ten list of operational priorities, as I once witnessed. You must play the game right, more so than anyone else. The alternative is a death knell.

It is comparable to being hunted. You may run, hide, or play dead. But you must stand up and be counted. And be proud of your accomplishments and commitment to the rules regardless of whether you are one hundred percent in agreement with each.

Think of compliance as a four-legged chair: one leg for federal, one for the state, one for accreditation, and one for your written policies. A campus of distinction works each day to keep all four legs of the compliance chair firm to the ground.

Your students deserve a commitment to quality. Your faculty and staff deserve it. The employers that hire your graduates deserve it. The investors, taxpayers, vendors, accreditors, and regulators deserve it. Play the game right and be accountable because you deserve it.

Recognition: Getting to Celebrate

When motivating teams and individuals, is there anything more powerful than formal or informal recognition of performance and notable efforts? Included are repeated acknowledgments of the accomplishments and struggles of students, faculty, and staff.

But there is one tenet that must be followed with diligence for recognition to become a proactive and motivating aspect of a people-intensive career education operation:

Praise in public. Reprimand in private.

Break the above rule just once with a student, employee, or coworker, and you will pay. Perhaps, we all have been victims of being praised anonymously in private and reprimanded unceremoniously in public.

Before praising or admonishing, remember how it feels, and you will do it right every time. Your team, campus, and the company will reap dividends from your kind approach to the everyday workplace habits of often praising in plain view and reprimanding—only when necessary—behind closed doors.

Of course, being part of a regulated business, you must be cognizant of incentives used as commendation symbols for students and employees. Sponsor awards ceremonies where you celebrate the individual, team, and class accomplishments. Quality plaques inscribed with thoughts of gratitude and consumables such as office and classroom supplies and study aids are worth the effort with nominal expenditures required.

Other examples of praising in public include a convenient parking space for a month; handwritten notes of thanks also shared with family, coworkers, and friends; or taking an entire team to lunch—must include everyone—although single out extraordinary individual performances when addressing the group with the obligatory thank you speech. Erect a wall of fame that displays, with their written permission, successful graduates with pride; or buy and serve the team, class, or student cohort a meal or a snack.

Use graduation ceremonies as an extension of your commitment to student-centered learning. Require students to wear caps and gowns, perhaps different colors for each academic or training program. Seat faculty and staff in support of the graduates, not above or in front as is typical at a traditional college ceremony.

Consider hiring a commencement speaker that students will relate to instead of your company's public relations department's politically motivated choice. Invest in your graduation ceremony. Hold it in a high-profile, convenient location. Decorate the event with class and dignity. Use current technology. Celebrate achievement.

And when your chief financial officer or business manager questions the line item merits of this budgeted expenditure, ask politely what they expect at a loved one's graduation.

Whether honoring students, alumni, faculty, staff, employers, or the families of each, celebrate success. Be creative. Be thankful. Be sincere. Be compliant. Do it in public. Do it often. I guarantee you will be renowned for your zeal to acknowledge successful efforts and compassionate contributions.

Institutional Quality Reflects a Positive Campus Climate

Corporate and regional managers; accreditors; and regulators who visit multiple campuses as part of regular job responsibilities have often shared that when entering a school, one can either cut the tension in the air with a knife or sense an aura of positive energy and professionalism. How does a perceptive visitor to your campus or office, online included, describe its kinesthetic atmosphere?

The principles discussed throughout *A Great Place to Learn & Earn* are about creating a campus or workplace that exudes a collaborative, positive, and ethical customer-centric culture. One that fosters an atmosphere of mutual trust, dignity, and respect, along with shared enthusiasm toward working together on a mission.

Partnering as a team by getting along, driving performance by getting it done, being compliant by getting it right, and remembering to distinguish your efforts by celebrating success, are paramount to pride and performance in the career education sector. These are the common traits found in high-achieving campuses and parent companies. Because each settles for nothing short of what faculty and staff work for—and students pay for—creating and maintaining a campus of distinction.

Four

HIRE TRAIN MONITOR MOTIVATE

TRAIN PEOPLE WELL ENOUGH TO LEAVE.
TREAT PEOPLE WELL ENOUGH NOT TO
WANT TO. —SIR RICHARD BRANSON

Student-centered, team-focused, and consensus-driven organizations in the career education sector share a commitment to excellence in recruiting and retaining faculty and staff that teach and serve its students. The unending responsibility is to hire, train, monitor, and motivate passionate employees focused on the desired student, campus, and company outcomes.

I was fortunate to serve successful tenures as director of admissions and campus president by learning and practicing the art of hiring, training, monitoring, and motivating. These four skills are necessary, in unison, to build and maintain a campus or company of distinction.

Hire for Attitude

As discussed in Chapter Two: People Before Vision and Chapter Three: Campus of Distinction, hiring the best talent possible is paramount to a successful organization. But this productive method of recruiting is counterintuitive to the conventional approach of focusing on qualifications and technical skills, a challenge in the credential-obsessed education field in general.

The key is to expand your search beyond the required checks and balances of matching candidates to accreditation or corporate human resource requirements. Hire qualified individuals with optimistic mind-sets, and you will build a team of greatness. Positive attitudes supply the needed fuel to winning teams.

Consider a different approach to group interviews. Turn the tables and first present your campus or company and its employment opportunity in a professional, entertaining format. Then allow your guests to sneak out of the building during a scheduled break if they determine the job or culture is not suitable. No hard feelings as you let everyone know in your opening statement that it is okay to exit with grace. The campus or company wishes everyone great success in their future career endeavors. For candidates who choose to return from the intermission, rest assured you have their undivided attention.

Now have each participant share with the entire group why they are the best candidate for the job opportunity presented and therefore deserve a scheduled formal interview. Then ask each candidate to vote for their choice in anonymity—it cannot be themselves—including a brief narrative on why. You will be amazed by the results.

I have hired some of my best employees from group interviews. The cream rises to the top. The winners are often spotted at the starting gate.

Alternatively, use the same presentation and approach in the one-on-one interview, granting the candidate permission to end the interview at any time if the opportunity is not as envisioned. If choosing to remain, as most will in the individual meeting format, have the interviewee explain at the close why they are the best fit for the job. Invite back those who impress for a second, more formal interview.

Once hired, the most dedicated employees will sometimes submit a letter of resignation because a once-in-a-lifetime opportunity found them that you were unable to match, or perhaps there is an unexpected spouse or partner relocation. Surprises such as these are why you need to be interviewing daily, regardless of openings. Or put another memorable way: *maintain blue suits in the lobby.*

Train for Quality

I have found a universal response to employee surveys is the perceived need for additional training. We are creatures of learning and thus have a perennial openness to further instruction, regardless of the level already offered. Therefore, whether a facilitator or a learner, it is crucial to remain in perpetual training mode.

But any employee training program in career education needs to focus on accreditation and regulatory requirements and individual and team performance toward expected student and institutional outcomes.

Group training sessions can be fun and productive for the education, financial aid, and business departments. Although admissions and career services teams enjoy group enlightenment, salespeople are susceptible to picking up bad habits in group learning paradigms. Therefore, it is recommended that admissions and career services personnel be limited to one-on-one training sessions with their supervisor.

Regardless, train for quality performance. Time constraints aside, learning opportunities are excellent vehicles for communicating goals and measuring outcomes that individuals and teams have committed to achieving, as well as a perfect opportunity to praise in public.

Hire quality people, and training sessions will become a rewarding get-together that celebrates success. The alternative is forced learning, with employees thinking why they checked "more training, please" on the survey in the first place.

When employees perceive training as a celebration of effort and an opportunity to learn things unknown, gatherings become popular events that inspire performance because of it as opposed to in spite of it.

Orientations are as crucial for new employees as for new students. The old cliché, first impressions are lasting, endures. It is recommended to have formal full-day new employee orientations with a written, segued agenda including interdepartmental participation. Once the new employee completes the required human resources paperwork, set them on a day to remember. Include an impassioned tour of relevant information and introductions. Take them to lunch. At the end of the day, leave the new employee thinking, "This is the best first day of work, ever!"

Monitor for Compliance

Contrary to conventional wisdom, most compliance issues in the career education sector result from unintentional negligence and under sight. Therefore, a compliance monitoring program designed and implemented to support and protect employees will be more efficient than one presented—or perceived—as a mere defense of the company's stock price or reputation.

Monitoring for compliance involves assisting faculty and staff in understanding and appreciating the myriad of regulations and accreditation criteria that forever loom over a campus or company. Employees often share, or think, what is not known is of most concern.

But in a culture of trust and understanding, preference is on learning what is not known. Mystery shops, corporate visits, and other forms of compliance monitoring become expected daily activities—not surprises—toward the mutual achievement of a squeaky clean, ethical and vibrant workplace.

Reward adherence to compliance in public, and coach shortcomings, in private. But make it part of the culture, thus eliminating the proverbial skeletons in the closet or eight hundred pound gorilla in the room.

Why do career education sector companies insist on employing campus directors of admissions and deans of education, but not local directors of compliance? Assuming the campus president is the director of compliance by default is a fiscal cop-out. And the notion of compliance is everyone's responsibility is also doomed to failure. When everyone is in charge, no one is in charge.

To illustrate the power of a director of compliance at the campus level, I once employed a gentleman in that role after being named the president of a degree-granting career school. He earned his annual salary early on by discovering two regulatory facts about our for-profit institution overlooked for decades.

One, the school was not subject to its then oversight by an onerous state regulatory agency whose purview was non-degree-granting for-profits. And two, as a degree-granting institution, we had the authority to use the word "college" in our name, considered impossible under previous corporate and campus interpretations of state legislation and regulations.

When we asked state officials why these two profound regulatory realities were not already in place, the answer was: "Because nobody ever challenged either one, no one ever asked." After filling out some forms and recording a sworn statement, we were granted college status under the authority of the state's higher education body that oversaw the traditional public and nonprofit colleges, including several world-renowned research universities.

Last I heard, this industrious director of compliance was working at an Ivy League school. Well done and deserved.

Monitor for compliance or be open to the observation of your relevant activities. Make it a priority. Make it fun. But do it. Your institution and its stakeholders are counting on you.

Motivate for Performance

Although necessary, motivating for performance is challenging in the current regulatory environment.

When the Obama administration removed the so-called twelve safe harbors of the incentive compensation clause within the Higher Education Act (HEA) in July 2011, enrollments at for-profit schools, colleges, and universities tumbled. Four years later, the sector's student populations remained well below record pre-2011 levels.

How did the removal of the safe harbors—thus making it illegal for institutions to reward faculty and staff for the enrollment, retention, and placement of students in specific ways—put the kibosh on the sector's growth?

A somewhat overlooked answer is the sector became too reliant on motivating staff toward the enrollment of new students, retaining active students, and the placement of graduates through incentives. These monetary inducements included graduation bonuses for admissions representatives, retention rewards for faculty, and placement bonuses for career services personnel.

Select employees—most often from admissions—were rewarded with dinners, elaborate trips, and other perks. Companies incentivized management with targeted annual bonus plans based on overall student and institutional outcomes.

For the most part, these plans were ethical, although inclined toward favoring new enrollment. In hindsight, career education sector companies missed the opportunity of distributing the safe harbor incentives across the outcomes spectrum of enrollment, financial aid, education, retention, receivables, and job placement.

One prominent U.S. senator, a Democrat, shared with me in a sidebar conversation, "We are not against for-profit education. We just have an issue with too much of the budget being spent on marketing and admissions." If any industry has painted a bull's eye on its back, it is the career education sector.

Now that the sow has been reaped, attention needs to focus on how to motivate—or be motivated—post twelve safe harbors. Here are ten best practices that ethical, high achieving department directors are implementing to keep staff inspired in the new regulatory climate:

1. Lunch when the entire team wins.
2. Awards ceremonies with approved plaques and trinkets.
3. Fun games for fueling the competitive spirit.
4. Frequent publication of privacy cleared student and institutional outcomes to sustain faculty and staff excitement about daily contributions.
5. Required faculty and staff attendance at graduation ceremonies to experience the meaning and ultimate joy of their work.
6. Graduating students and alumni, as speakers, at the heart of the commencement agenda.
7. Publish and distribute privacy cleared dean's lists, allowing faculty and staff to congratulate the honored students.
8. Schedule events outside of campus to engage with the public by promoting what you do well.
9. Conduct student surveys to not only correct common denominator issues but to share with faculty, staff, and corporate the positive things students say about the campus and its dedicated employees.
10. Remember to praise in public and reprimand in private.

Apply these and other motivational tools to each department, including admissions, financial aid, the business office, education, career or student services, and the campus management team. The twelve safe harbors are gone, although the ability to motivate in ethical ways remains critical to sustaining the career education sector's role in twenty-first century workforce development.

Hire, Train, Monitor, and Motivate for Results

When putting people first—students in particular—a career education operation will assimilate to a culture that hires employees for positive attitudes in addition to the required credentials. When there are no openings, interview blue suits to maintain bench strength.

Train for quality performance, starting with a world-class new employee orientation day, keeping in mind training is an individual exercise as much as a group one. Monitor for compliance to laws, regulations, accreditation standards, and company policies in a non-threatening manner. Share a commitment to following the rules by first knowing what the rules are. Motivate for performance through prescribed efforts to acknowledge, then reinforce, employee and student strengths. And tolerate any shortcomings that are not otherwise liabilities of the institution.

Applying these and other time-tested principles with consistency, and being open to receiving them, will more often lead to prosperous and ethical outcomes.

Now recite and repeat: hire, train, monitor, motivate.

Five

PLAYING THE GAME THE RIGHT WAY

LEARN THE RULES OF THE GAME. THEN PLAY THE GAME BETTER THAN ANYONE ELSE. —ALBERT EINSTEIN

A straightforward question for any campus or corporate employee, whether faculty, staff, administrator, or senior executive: "Assuming genuine interest exists in the corresponding career, and at full tuition, would you enroll your child or other loved one, in any of your school or company's programs?"

If the answer is a resounding "yes," the remainder of this chapter is a recap of what you already know. Hesitation in answering the question is a call for action.

A successful career education sector program, campus, or company of distinction embraces five cultural realities essential for long-term sustainability:

- New student enrollment drives the institution.
- Academic quality defines the institution.
- Collecting tuition makes paydays possible.
- Regulatory compliance: do it right or game over.

■ Graduate placement rate is the ultimate report card.

A career education culture that subscribes to these five mantras at the program, campus, and corporate levels is—as they say in professional baseball—playing the game the right way. Delivering operational excellence across departments is critical to sheer survival. Just as in competitive sports, elite performance begins with first understanding and then mastering the fundamentals.

New Student Enrollment Drives the Institution

At a tuition-dependent school, college, or university, nothing happens until somebody enrolls. Financial aid cannot package students, nor education teach or train. The business office cannot collect tuition, nor career services place graduates in jobs. And the administration cannot manage its budget in real-time unless the admissions team enrolls new students.

The relentless driving of enrollment has been the doom of some career education sector operations. One premise of *A Great Place to Learn & Earn* is suggesting a return, or perhaps first visit, to legacy enrollments. What if high quality, low price academic or training programs created active student, alumni, or employer generated new student referrals, thus putting a substantial dent in the stereotypical twenty-five percent marketing and admissions budgets?

One may argue that driving enrollment keeps a tuition-dependent institution in business. But exhausting one-quarter of revenue on this activity is perhaps the leading cause of the sector's precipitous downfall. Sometimes you must take one step back to go two steps forward.

In my first job as an admissions representative at Katharine Gibbs, we were trained from the premise of screening prospective students as future workers for our base of employers. This enrollment model dictated that an admissions representative's first loyalty was to the organizations that hired our graduates. The primary goal was to recruit students who were believed potential candidates to represent the school well in the eyes of employers, deemed the ultimate customer.

To be recommended to a program, prospective students had to demonstrate interest, desire, and motivation for the particular career being sought. Missing was the training provided to successful candidates in exchange for tuition, although with no guarantee of employment.

Accepting enrollment agreements at the initial interview was rare. Prospective students without an earned bachelor's degree were scheduled to return at a specific date and time to take an admissions test. Those who passed the assessment were then permitted to enroll and pay the required fee. Closing rate, i.e., enrollments to interviews, was lower than industry standards; although the start rate, i.e., new student starts to enrollments was higher than industry averages.

Under this format, I progressed to where fifty percent of my interviews were starting school, and of those that matriculated, seventy-six percent were graduating. My performance was representative of overall company improvement in enrollment and retention that occurred right after the 1992 reauthorization of the Higher Education Act (HEA), which eliminated the paying of commissions for the recruitment of students. Nonetheless, it was a successful admissions model both in quantity and quality.

What if the career education sector returned to similar ways of ethical enrolling or invented new methodologies? I learned that less was more as far as producing higher graduation, job placement, and loan repayment rates.

Reverting to legacy enrollment—as opposed to the current strategy of buying new students via web initiatives—is paramount to a quality admissions process. At Katharine Gibbs, we produced significant unsolicited referrals of new students from active students, graduates, and employers. This methodology also generated referrals from students that canceled or dropped, another testament to the perceived value in this principled approach to admissions, supported by quality career training.

Cost-effective lead generation and ethical new student enrollment from marketing and admissions drive the institution, allowing everyone else to perform the essential work of teaching and serving willing students.

Academic Quality Defines the Institution

In one of his earlier interviews upon taking over Apple, for the second time, the late Steve Jobs said his commitment to developing cutting-edge devices was putting the product before the process. His emphasis was on the merits of the product and the people who designed it instead of corporate process or procedure. Considering the infamous products Apple has introduced since that interview in the mid-1990s, Jobs's theory worked.

Because of the myriad of regulations and accreditation standards that it faces, postsecondary career education has become a process-driven sector, thus putting its educational products on the back burner. New enrollment, financial aid packaging, regulatory compliance, expense management, tuition collection, syllabi adherence, human resource policies, student retention, and other process-directed activities can undermine the critical role that quality academic or training programs play in a thriving career education culture.

New or revised curriculum delivered to the institution's door in a box, thus requiring a limited local contribution, has become the norm. However, despite being a standard of accreditation, faculty involvement in program development is often orchestrated at the bare minimum.

But an institution or company's reputation in the community is about the quality of its program offerings. Curricula that is up-to-date and delivered with excellence impresses upon students, employers, regulators, and accreditors; and breeds positive influence on elected officials, mainstream media, and the public.

Institutions or programs that focus on quality products and delivery develop exceptional reputations for the school, college, university, or company. When product quality is ignored or discounted, troubling times are often close behind. Perhaps the new standard of the career education sector will be putting quality academic programs above all else. A significant positive reinvention of the sector's reputation lies in the balance.

Collecting Tuition Makes Paydays Possible

Any business or organization, regardless of tax status, relies on collecting receivables for financial survival. In postsecondary career education, collecting tuition, whether in the form of federal or state financial aid proceeds, scholarship dollars, or cash payments from students, is the lifeblood of the organization's existence as a sound economic entity.

The regulatory and procedural responsibility of collecting and posting tuition is assigned to the business office, or equivalent, although it is everyone's business. Collecting tuition makes paydays possible. For this reason, each employee of a career sector school, college, or university, is in some way accountable for receivables. To be sure, processing and posting actual collections is limited to sanctioned personnel; however, other faculty and staff are role players by default.

Ensuring a student gets to the business or bursar's office, whether on ground or online; establishing the importance of student financial responsibility in each department; and being an enthusiastic player in what is often uncomfortable for faculty and staff, goes far in contributing to the fiscal strength of the career education organization. Just as important is the financial well-being of the student.

Administrative capability in Title IV processing, combined with ethical collection activity—and happy students—often leads to low bad debt, a revealing financial indicator of a rigorous career education operation. Participation from faculty and staff at approved levels is a predictive indicator of a sound collection process.

Conversations in the student lounge, or online forum, mirrors the perception of a collections process's strength and dignity. If students sense a disciplined, consistent, and ethical approach, the word will spread to keep your account current, or else no more dream of a career. On the contrary, lack of discipline, consistency, or ethics in the collection process leads to complacency among students.

When confronted with the opportunity to assist in the collection process, think of that student's career dream and your paycheck. Collecting tuition makes both possible.

Regulatory Compliance: Do It Right or Game Over

Live by the sword or die by the sword is an ageless expression anchored in the career education sector. Here the sword is federal Title IV authorization and the student funding it propels. These taxpayer-driven dollars are relied upon by tuition-dependent schools, colleges, and universities, regardless of the institution's tax status.

The one who holds the gold makes the rules is another timeless and relevant axiom. It is analogous to the federal government's oversight of an eligible institution's awarding and dispersing taxpayer-funded student financial aid. Demonstrate negligence, even if not deliberate, and it is game over for the guilty school, college, or university. Operations that are in noncompliance with state regulations and institutional or programmatic accreditation lay victim to this potential death knell as well. The message is clear: play the game right or stop playing the game.

Regulatory compliance in all its forms—federal, state, local, accreditation, and an institution's written policy—forever remains in the organization's consciousness. To live with the benefits of the rules, you are indoctrinated to play by the rules. It is well defined, and for the most part, not negotiable.

As suggested in Chapter Four: Hire Train Monitor Motivate, assign a director of compliance to each location as a permanent footprint to your institution's operating model. Proclaim the existence of the director of compliance as worthy of the traditional roles of campus president and directors of admission, financial aid, education, business, and career services.

Arguably, the career education sector's maligned history has been recorded from under sight in regulatory compliance. Granted, these were unintended misdeeds—limited to a few bad actors in the sector—but negligence nonetheless in oversight due to naiveté, lack of resources, or misguided budgeting priorities. A dedicated, on-site compliance manager might curtail findings of noncompliance to levels never before thought possible. The alternative is the proverbial penny-wise but dollar foolish omission, a practice all too common in the sector.

As the sector reinvents itself as an ethical contributor to workforce development, the inclusion of sustainable regulatory compliance expenditures in annual budgets will be crucial to reversing negative perceptions, or worse, damaging audits. Delivering regulatory department budget lines with a percentage weighting equitable to admissions, student finance, education, and career services, may be the difference between notable success, mere survival, or inescapable demise.

Similar to any industry grounded by a clear and decisive set of rules and regulations—think law, accounting, alcoholic beverages, commercial aviation, energy, and defense—the choice is clear: play by the rules or be ejected from the game. Questioning non-negotiable laws, regulations, standards, or policies is a fool's game. Following them is an act of outright survival.

Make the management of regulatory compliance a priority. Students and other stakeholders will benefit from this renewed commitment to playing the game the right way.

Graduate Placement Rate is the Ultimate Report Card

The career education sector has one universal mission: job training for interested students. Career level employment is a definitive student outcome, whether academic or skilled or entry-level or promotion, and the primary reason for the sector's existence as specialty education providers in the first place. Therefore, upon graduation and beyond, the student placement rate is the ultimate report card on an institution or company's performance.

Some in the sector deem gainful employment regulations a nuisance, perhaps an overreach by the federal government or an industry-targeted sabotage attempt. But what if accreditors and regulators are forced to up the ante on defining an acceptable placement? I submit suitable employment lies in the eyes of the beholders: the graduate and the employer. Is the job consistent with the original or renewed motivation behind the student's enrollment? Does it fulfill the specific needs of the employer? If a concurrent yes, you have the fundamental underpinnings of gainful employment.

Nevertheless, if government intervention is the primary solution to ethical employment outcomes of paying students and supporting taxpayers, then conventional placement verifications such as five-day qualifiers, temporary work, and part-time jobs may go by the wayside.

Regardless, if the student and the employer achieve reasonable expectations from the outset in joint partnership with the institution—regulatory burdens notwithstanding—a successful placement has been made. Hence, an end game of mutual student and employer perceived gainful employment, combined with renewed regulator and accreditor placement qualifiers, puts the career education sector back in the driver's seat as the primary source for job training.

If you cannot defeat it, i.e., the federal government, and cannot, or refuse to join, i.e., traditional public and nonprofit higher education, surprise each with the equivalent of straight A's on this ultimate report card of performance. In postsecondary career education, that equates to superior placement opportunities and outcomes for willing and able graduates of its institutions, thereby yielding a mutual benefit to employers and the community.

Individuals Playing as One College Team

In its simplest form, the sport of baseball comprises a group of statistics-driven individual athletes finding ways to play as a team to win games and championships. Career education is no different.

The sector's stakeholders are measured for individual performance but must play the game the right way by working together as one college team. By driving enrollment, financing students, developing and delivering educational products and student services, collecting tuition, managing regulations and accreditation standards, and placing graduates or completers in gainful employment, the opportunity is created for the team and the individual to win the game.

The new standard in the career education sector is to play the game with passion and the will to win, coupled with a renewed ethical approach and lifelong commitment to sustainable workforce development in the greater public interest.

Six

STAKEHOLDER DRIVEN
DECISION MAKING

*WHENEVER YOU SEE A SUCCESSFUL BUSI-
NESS, SOMEONE ONCE MADE A COURA-
GEOUS DECISION.* —PETER F. DRUCKER

Successful career education organizations balance seven interested stakeholders. Companies and campuses of distinction make key tactical and strategic decisions based on what is best for the institution and its primary participants.

The Seven Principal Stakeholders of the Career Education Sector:

- Students, including alumni, the paying customers, and lifelong ambassadors.
- Faculty and staff, the employees that teach and support students.
- Employers that hire graduates and come back again if the institution trains well.
- Ownership, or shareholders, that provide needed capital infusion.
- Corporate, or front office that operates the institution on behalf of ownership.
- Vendors that deliver essential academic and operational products and services.

- Community, including legislators, regulators, accreditors, and independent board or advisory members that oversee the institution in the public interest.

A long-standing sector decree says the student comes first. But this doctrine may be challenged if situations dictate that by putting other stakeholders foremost, students benefit.

One example is a new regulation or standard that is unpopular with students yet not negotiable. Implement by explaining to students *the why* behind the action without throwing the third party overseer under the bus. In the eyes of students and other stakeholders, comprehending the why often trumps non-acceptance. Although disapproving of the verdict, most will concede when reaching a level of understanding.

Another example of putting other stakeholders before the student is when prospective students' admission is denied to a particular program due to space constraints as engineered by active shareholders and corporate executives. Redesigning the curriculum before a cohort graduates to satisfy renewed employer demands—perhaps recommended by the program advisory board—may also come into play. Community-sponsored certification testing requirements may give the appearance of placing students second, although in the spirit of protecting the public trust.

One may argue the above examples are purposeful in placing the student; first, something ethical stakeholders and interested observers can support and embrace.

Whether at the corporate, campus management, or academic program level, it is good practice to consider the benefits and possible consequences to the seven principal stakeholders when making major decisions, developing strategic plans, designing curriculum, or crafting mission statements. And it is advisable to include other relevant stakeholders, where and when practical, before reaching decisions or implementing strategies.

In traditional public and nonprofit higher education, processes have built-in mechanisms that trigger required stakeholder input, often called shared governance. Similar horizontal approaches to hierarchy are practiced less within the for-profit business model. However, incorporating students, faculty, and other stakeholders into vertical decision lines can produce an equal perception of inclusion, thereby contributing to a harmonious and productive workplace.

It's About Everyone's Career

Working in career education is a commitment to partnership, involving mutual trust and respect for everyone's job, whether that of a student, faculty or staff member, employer, owner or investor, corporate staffer or senior manager, vendor, or legislator, regulator, or accreditor.

Implement the following paradigm into your institution or company's culture, and I guarantee it will harvest improvement of stakeholder retention and satisfaction never thought possible:

- Every day, give the students a reason to come back tomorrow
- Every day, give each other a reason to come back tomorrow

Consider redesigning your operational model to respect the careers of the sector's seven principal stakeholders. Rest assured each will be grateful for the deliberate inclusion.

Develop Compelling Strategies

Institutional accreditation standards require mission statements. Vision statements are also a good practice. The right people, including interested stakeholders, are necessary ingredients to developing strategies that will transform and sustain your organization as a great place to learn and earn.

Practice good leadership when implementing strategies, missions, or visions by supporting teaching and learning, student services, regulatory compliance, stakeholder inclusion, and appropriate celebrations.

- Commit to faculty professional development as a benefit, not a privilege.
- Foster student learning with intensive tutoring and personal support services.
- Sponsor a legitimate staff development program.
- Cultivate branded employer partnerships promoted in the community.
- Hold vendors accountable, albeit treat each as a valued stakeholder.
- Drive and reward a culture of compliance, integrity, and ethics.
- Celebrate success, often and in public, for students, faculty, and staff.
- Schedule regular all-staff meetings with approved awards at every level:
    - Ownership
    - Corporate
    - Campus
    - Program
    - Faculty
    - Department
    - Staff

Any holistic approach to strategic development that embraces and rewards participation from each of the seven stakeholders will, more often than not, yield a campus or company of distinction.

Define Your Economic Driver

Because of general dissonance toward making a profit from postsecondary education, the public disregards the interconnected economic model in the career education sector that drives mutually dependent bottom lines of student outcomes and institutional profitability.

Mutually Dependent Bottom Lines:

- The student is pursuing program completion toward permanent gainful employment.
- The institution is pursuing student outcomes toward sustainable profitability.

In for-profit career education, one bottom line cannot be obtained ethically without the other. If students are graduating and obtaining gainful employment, the institution will recognize profits, assuming sound fiscal management. And by reinvesting a reasonable portion of the profits back into the operation's capital structure, more students will have the opportunity to graduate and be placed. Although counterintuitive in its dynamic, this mutual dependence of outcomes and profitability is a valuable starting point in defining your organization's economic engine. In today's challenging regulatory climate, it may be necessary to ramp up the motor by adding several additional cylinders.

One example is a per program requirement of double-digit profit margins, minimum seventy percent achievement in student retention and graduate placement, less than twenty percent cohort default rate, and meeting federal gainful employment metrics. Further, if a program fails to meet each driver regularly as prescribed, it becomes a candidate to teach out. Potential new training or academic programs undergoing feasibility must demonstrate that specified reasonable outcomes are attainable before any applications are submitted for approvals to roll out.

Strong enrollment potential is not an excuse to ignore appropriate capital availability measures, projected student retention, employer demand, and gainful employment potential. Regulatory compliance, combined with the program's likelihood of approval, forecasted graduate placement rates, expected gainful employment outcomes, capital requirements, and the availability of qualified faculty and staff to teach and manage the program, are paramount to its holistic, sustainable success.

How often do career education institutions make chicken, a favorite expression in the fast-food business, where a new menu item rolls out because the restaurant across the street is already offering it? Companies and campuses make chicken by introducing new programs born of limited feasibility based on enrollment potential, competitive threats, or employer demand. These programs are produced lightning fast with template-driven corporate, state, accreditation, and federal approval applications. The results are new offerings that attract scores of students but limited employer interest, or just as frustrating, high employer demand, yet negligible enrollment.

In today's regulatory environment, more than ever, the sector needs to rebuild its economic engine to one that encompasses key drivers necessary for maintaining successful career training or academic degree programs. A sample educational program specific mission statement:

> Predictable enrollment potential supported by real-time outcomes assessment or comprehensive feasibility that demonstrates the program is approval worthy, has affordable tuition, sufficient staffing capability, acceptable retention, substantial

placement potential based on verified employer demand, is gainful employment manageable, and has an adequate capital investment.

Any program failing to deliver mandated qualifiers measured with
minimal institutional, accreditation, and regulatory standards is a candidate to teach out; or is denied at the planning stage due to insufficient
feasibility.

Quality Begets Quantity

It is perhaps the sector's responsibility, in the interest of the seven principal stakeholders, to offer career and academic programs that produce
targeted quantity by way of quality, as opposed to the more common
inverse approach of quantity first. Filling seats and then practicing crisis
intervention to overcome higher than expected student populations or
difficult to reach outcomes is a fool's game in the career education sector.

Failed practices at the hands of overzealous practitioners that rea-
soned quantity invoked quality inhabit institution and program grave-
yards. But perhaps these resting places of the sector's worse days are
becoming overshot with uncut grass and wilted flowers, a welcomed re-
prieve allowing the sector's seven deserved stakeholders an opportunity
to be active, valued players in the twenty-first century's workforce development.

Seven

HELLO ZONES AND MORE SIMPLE RULES FOR EVERYDAY SUCCESS

SUCCESS IS A CHOICE. —RICK PITINO

In the quest to play the game the right way, teams or individuals adhere to a defined set of rules that apply to specific organizations and industries. I have uncovered a handful of simple rules common to postsecondary career education that goes far in defining a culture of distinction. Indeed, each may be modified to fit a corporate, campus, or online environment.

Hello Zones

How often do you pass a student, colleague, or visitor in the hallway only to find that person looking down or away? In high school, you may have succumbed to insecurities in a similar moment and concluded you were unworthy. Comparable interaction in postsecondary education is often a sign the passerby is the one lacking confidence or self-esteem. It is thereby an inherited obligation of stakeholders in the sector to transform common areas into *hello zones*.

In a hello zone culture, faculty and staff must acknowledge those with whom paths cross, regardless of whether they are students, colleagues, or visitors. Simple eye contact, accompanied by a warm and enthusiastic hello, will inspire the unassuming partner to raise their head and return the gesture. If the person is already known, expand the hello zone by engaging with appropriate comments or questions based on mutual understanding.

I implemented hello zones at several inherited campuses and was thrilled by the positive energy levels developed in the common areas. It seems contrived when first shared with a new employee during orientation, although it works. I have never heard a single complaint about the hello zones.

If not already practicing this cultural wake-up protocol, begin today. You will be amazed at the results. Regardless, the hello zone plays a role in employer demanded soft skills training for students. At job interviews, graduates of hello zone campuses are naturals at keeping their heads up and eyes forward.

Operate hello zones, and experience the joy of a parent or loved one approaching you at graduation to share how confident and communicative the student has become since attending your school. Such gestures are a testament to the dedicated work of faculty and staff. The hello zones support those efforts. They work wonders.

Campus Safety and Security

Does your campus or office suite require photo identification for on-site students and employees? A mandatory sign-in and pass procedure for visitors? How about security personnel equipped with video software to monitor the comings and goings during hours of operation? Does your campus or workplace maintain a camera and motion security system with central monitoring when closed? How about a safety and security committee that convenes on a regular timetable? And how would you rate your online security software and monitoring system as far as preventing hacking, harassment, or cheating?

To be sure, the federal government triggers some of these security measures as mandated by the Clery Act. But I was once confronted by two separate and stark reminders, in a single day, on why campus security is as important as quality education and profitable operations.

On the morning of April 16, 2007, I was in my office serving as executive director of a growing career training school when I saw the tragic news flash on the internet that gunfire had killed thirty-two persons and wounded seventeen others at Virginia Polytechnic Institute and State University, also known as Virginia Tech. The perpetrator was a lone gunman, a senior student at the university with a mental illness history.

Later that morning, a dental assistant student entered my office inquiring about security procedures on our campus. I responded with empathy, expressing the horror of the Virginia Tech shooting, that I understood her concerns, and assured her the school acts out of safety first for our students, faculty, and staff. She looked confused as she responded, "Oh my god, I had no idea, that is horrible, but the reason for my visit is I was just in the student lounge buying something from a vending machine when I felt a tap on my shoulder. I turned around, and it was my ex-boyfriend." He was not a student at the school.

Startled by this related and shocking concern, I sprang from my seat and assisted the student in her time of need. Everything worked out as her ex-boyfriend left with no incident. With a renewed sense of urgency, I convened the campus safety and security committee that proceeded to implement unprecedented measures. The updated plan included a photo identification of students and employees; a sign-in/sign-out procedure for visitors and vendors; uniformed security personnel at open-access entrances; online video surveillance; and an electronic fob system where those authorized with coded keys opened the exterior doors of the building. Doors opened unencumbered from the inside to facilitate emergency exiting.

Although some of these new security measures were not budgeted, there was no objection from a just as concerned corporate office.

Several months later, an epilogue to this story occurred when I obtained a well-written nineteen-page manual courtesy of Virginia Tech titled, *How to Respond to Disruptive or Threatening Student Behavior*. This informative report's tragic irony is the University published it two years before the horrific mass shooting.

In career education, we are fortunate to operate in a closed campus society instead of the typical open society environments of traditional college campuses such as Virginia Tech. I had reminded faculty and staff about our willingness and ability to remove an unstable student or employee from the school long before they become a severe threat to our well-being. Upgrading our campus safety and security, post-Virginia Tech, was our responsibility as well, as we inherited a newfound commitment to not taking anything for granted.

Having occurred two years after the university wrote a manual for dealing with troubled students, the Virginia Tech shooting provokes the twofold importance of having a plan and working the plan. The tragedy further reminds us that well-intentioned plans are vulnerable. Another blunt reminder that you must have a comprehensive security blueprint in place, regardless. Please do it for your students, employees, and visitors; and in memory and honor of the forty-nine victims and their families, friends, and colleagues at Virginia Tech.

Lights On

When visiting a retail store during hours of operation, it is rare to encounter a department with its lights turned off. Nonetheless, why is it common to see the lights off in some physical campus areas during classroom and office hours? I am a proponent of energy conservation for both environmental and financial reasons. But students, employees, and visitors deserve a well-lit, open for learning and business environment.

The lights-on rule is sympathetic to evening students and visitors who often enter a building of vacated classrooms, labs, offices, and common areas — some darkened from the learned habit of turning lights off and closing the door behind. To supersede this tendency, implement a rule of thumb where those approved to open and close the campus each day have exclusive control of the lighting.

Walk Directions

When a new student, employee, or visitor asks for directions to a lab, the business office, or a bathroom, walk them as opposed to offering the confusing, "Go down there and make your second right into the hallway at the Graduate Hall of Fame, then at the accreditation commendation plaque make a left, and the classroom you are looking for is the third door on the right. To be sure, check that it is Room Number 22 before you enter to confirm you are in the correct place."

The example is an exaggeration, but if left to navigate alone, you can bet the student, employee, or visitor will be asking for directions again on the way. Walk the person or group to the destination and use the journey as an opportunity for a productive conversation. Everyone will feel better for it. Make this a campus-wide rule. Stakeholder value points are guaranteed to tick up on surveys from this act of genuine customer service.

Walk directions is another rule common to ground operations, although it may be tailored online with mandatory follow-up mechanisms after providing electronic instructions on request.

Return Student Communications Within 24 Hours

Interacting with students outside of the classroom has taken many forms in the information age: voice mail, texts, emails, online forums, website inquiries, social media, and other electronic vehicles. A mandatory twenty-four-hour return rule creates urgency. Better yet, make it the same day or same hour, or same minute for that matter, considering today's instantaneous world created by the internet and smartphones.

I had an admissions team that, each evening and weekend, sent a company-owned smartphone home with an anointed admissions representative to respond real-time to online inquiries. Technology providers now market interactive smartphone software for a more systematic approach to electronic student communication.

Perhaps the day is near where every department is armed with campus-owned smartphones with intelligent apps to ensure prompt communication at each level of the student timeline. It makes good technical sense as a renewed competitive edge. At a minimum, it projects customer service savvy in the rapid-response world of the twenty-first century.

Automatic replies generated during off-hours have become compulsory, although each inquiry needs to be returned by a live human being at some point. And automatic responses to prospective students should never be substituted for a person in real-time during regular business hours.

Regardless of the student's chosen vehicle, return the communication within twenty-four hours, or better yet, in a New York minute.

Be Wary of Airing Dirty Laundry in the Presence of Students

In the privacy-sensitive world of education, being cognizant of what is shared in public is compulsory, requiring an astute sense of space as worthy discussions about students are frequent among faculty and staff.

Consider implementing training guidance of looking over both shoulders, closing the door if appropriate, and being conscious of who is in earshot before embarking on a meaningful and legal conversation to benefit the student customer in focus. Strong privacy-sensitive institutions also remind students to practice earshot maintenance before engaging in otherwise appropriate discussions about others.

A wonderful thing about career training is the education is perpetual and seamless throughout the student's enrollment timeline. How students act in the classroom, hallway, parking lot, or online forum will often translate to the professional workplace. Teach well, and lead by example.

Under Promise, Then Over Deliver

I made a habit of asking students about their overall experience at the school or how the current course was progressing. The answer often was, "It is better than I thought it was going to be." A welcomed reminder that faculty and staff were promising the student enough to stay motivated without the student being set up for later disappointment.

Whether participating in the admissions interview, financial aid process, new student orientation, syllabus review on the first day of a course, entertaining student questions in the business office, or conducting a mock interview or resume review in career services, search for ways to under-promise, thus allowing your colleagues in the program, department, campus, or company to over-deliver. It is an art requiring training and practice that is guaranteed to provide dividends in student satisfaction and regulatory compliance.

Your colleagues will admire and thank you for your modest contribution of under-promising, thereby permitting each to over-deliver. Corporate personnel, regulators, and accreditors recognize institutions that practice this rule for everyday success. Students may not be aware of being under-promised and over-delivered the education or services on a conscious level. However, they will sense something positive is happening.

Transform Students to Raving Fans

If the definition of good customer service is going above and beyond to assist a student, then the definition of great customer service is:

> Going above and beyond for the student with genuine enjoyment.

I often agree with colleagues in postsecondary career education that our sector is not suitable for the faint of heart. As discussed in Chapter Three: Campus of Distinction, assertive, self-motivated, and customer intensive professionals that possess a strong work ethic are the most successful performers in the sector. But a genuine approach to customer service is crucial to this simple rule for everyday success. If assisting students in enrolling, financing, learning, or placing is performed without intentional care and empathy, working in postsecondary career education is a stressful and challenging job, indeed.

You engage in real-time with your customers more so than most other industries. Genuine enjoyment of the experience, whether a good day or a bad day for the employee or student, is a foundation for lifelong success in career-focused education. Love it or leave it as the saying goes, although choosing to stay should be inspired by an appreciation for the career training culture. You are changing lives for the better, including your own.

But customer service in the career education sector is about more than being nice. Maintaining professionalism is expected, although empathy will often trump sympathy. For example, as a new director of admissions, I met with a prospective student on behalf of an admissions representative because the student had enrolled and then canceled her application for the third time without completing the financial aid process. I had a frank conversation with the student about how not following through was perhaps affecting her entire life. And although I understood her fear of the financial aid process based on what could go wrong with eligibility, in general, to cancel without the facts amounted to self-sabotage on her part.

The prospective student proceeded to get defensive, accusing me of being interested in her starting school because that was my job. I responded by sharing that I already had a career, so this was not about me as much as her obtaining a job. And I meant every word of it. At that point, she left my office without saying goodbye and proceeded out of the building.

I informed the admissions representative that I was not successful in saving her student. But several minutes later, as I was looking down at my desk, I felt a presence in front of me. When I looked up, lo and behold, it was the same prospective student. She sat down and volunteered that she had been sitting in her car thinking about our discussion and that she was adverse to follow through. She shared that I was the first person ever to confront her about these fears and how she was letting them stop her from pursuing the dream of an honorable career.

In the end, she scheduled a financial aid appointment, attended orientation, started school, graduated, and was placed in a full-time position by career services. I had been fortunate to learn in my career that empathy and genuine customer service drive career education. And as the new director of admissions at that particular campus, a bonus was the good first impression conveyed on the team that day. In my mind, the student was the clear winner from the honest interaction; and that is what counted most.

Practice What You Preach and Teach

What is preached and taught in the students' presence is expected behavior from staff and faculty in career education.

Whether an on-ground classroom or online platform, having well-defined students' rules is paramount to effective academic delivery and classroom control toward positive outcomes. But, in students' eyes, published decrees in course syllabi and student handbooks become meaningless if influential stakeholders violate similar pronouncements. Below is a shortlist of traditions practiced by faculty, staff, and students at institutions playing the game the right way.

- Good attendance
- On-time performance
- Positive attitude
- Professional appearance
- Organized work area
- Cleanliness and hygiene
- Teamwork and collaboration
- Ethical service
- Lifelong learning

A typical student in postsecondary career education may score lower on college preparatory exams such as the SAT® or ACT® than a successful traditional higher education student. But if you could administer a consumer aptitude test on street smarts, the career sector student might outdo the traditional college-bound scholar. Therefore, remain on your toes after setting ground rules with your students. You will be flatfooted when called out for behavior to the contrary.

Practice what you preach and teach for a harmonious and productive campus of distinction.

Simple Rules Make Success a Welcomed Choice

Developing and administering a clear set of simple rules for campus constituents to adhere to is essential in a career-focused, open enrollment environment. Faculty and staff are thankful for an organized workplace; students for institutional consistency; employers for the dedication to soft skills; vendors for appropriate use of products and services; and regulators and accreditors for the devotion to compliance produced as a result.

Nevertheless, some personalities polarize anything labeled a rule. Call it something else if deemed necessary by the institutional culture. In the spirit of stakeholder-driven decision-making, how about *the art of fairness and inclusion*?

Eight

NAVIGATING THE HIGHER EDUCATION INDUSTRIAL COMPLEX

ONE OF THE GREATEST OBSTACLES TO ES-CAPING POVERTY IS THE STAGGERING COST OF HIGHER EDUCATION. —THE HONORABLE U.S. SENATOR CHRIS VAN HOLLEN

During his farewell address to the nation on January 17, 1961, General Dwight D. Eisenhower—the retiring two-term U.S. president and World War II hero—warned the United States citizens about the *military-industrial complex.*

According to Eisenhower, the military-industrial complex comprises the policy and monetary relationships at the federal level between legislators, the armed forces, defense contractors, and the president as commander-in-chief. During his speech, Eisenhower said, "We must guard against the acquisition of unwarranted influence, whether sought or unsought, by the military-industrial complex." Today, it may be argued his warning has gone unheeded.

Similar in scope, the *higher education industrial complex* comprises state and federal legislators and regulators; public, nonprofit, and for-profit educational institutions and organizations; policy think tanks; and mainstream media. On the one hand, this diverse and collective influence has created a higher education model of global envy. On the other, it is an excessive and inflationary force, exerting tremendous influence despite serving less than one-third of adult Americans when measuring earned degrees at the bachelor's level or higher. An ever-growing international student population exacerbates the controversy among protectionists.

In personal observations, some players in the higher education industrial complex's traditional arm continue to protect the previous century's status quo of competitive admissions, on-ground learning, faculty-centric governance, and tax-exempt status. It comes at the expense of much-needed progress and change in this century through cost controls and efficient use of technology, even if disruptive. But the good news is status quo seldom prevails in a progressive society. If it did, we might still be in a primitive state of existence.

In this essay-themed chapter, I have compiled my public comments from the past several years to illustrate one insider's view on this dynamic state of American higher education today and its impact on the career education sector's survival and continued role in workforce development. I offer a counterpoint to the higher education industrial complex, whether public, nonprofit, or for-profit. Opinions are my own.

On Gainful Employment and the 90/10 Rule

Gainful employment is applied predominantly and 90/10 regulations exclusively to for-profit, tax-generating institutions. As a taxpayer, I am not opposed to applying both rules to every Title IV authorized school, college, or university.

According to gainful employment regulation authors and supporters, degree-granting programs at nonprofit and state-owned colleges and universities should not be held accountable for graduates' gainful employment. A stark reminder of the disparity between traditional colleges and their students: the former presumes each enrolls merely to be educated. The latter believe they enrolled to learn and obtain a career. The traditional institutions are winning the argument.

How many students in higher education are indeed attending for the primary goal of gainful employment upon graduation? The corresponding regulations are a grudging attack on open-admission schools that cater to the nation's less fortunate. Who else will serve these millions of students? I envision the unintended consequence of this elitist assault on the career education sector is the growing cohort of low-income or ill-prepared students that the for-profits now serve will become the ultimate victims due to limited access to career training.

The failed gainful employment lobby from the sector now resembles a mid-semester term paper compared to what the nonprofits must have thrown at the Obama administration to water down its college accountability initiative from a prescriptive rating system to the mere consumer information website.

Nonetheless, the for-profit sector must adapt to gainful employment regulations with strategic workforce partnerships, something a typical community college excels at negotiating and publicizing. However, it struggles to execute based on low average graduation rates. If history is any guide, being less prone to slow-moving, bureaucratic, and politicized cultures, the career education sector will deliver.

Gainful employment could relegate job training back to the employers, raising consumer prices to pay for the added costs of doing business. How would you react if the dental assistant working on your teeth told you they were hired and trained off *craigslist*? Such dilemmas are starting to sound like Yogi Berra's "déjà vu all over again," as hiring and training from classified ads was the norm before postsecondary schools started vocational training programs such as dental assisting; in this case, to the delight of dentists and unknowing patients everywhere. So much for progress.

Gainful employment's singular focus on programs that attract a predominance of low-income students is another reminder that U.S. higher education is an unleveled playing field. The affluent individual attends the traditional four-year college; the low-income person goes to the community college or for-profit, often both, in that order.

Since state university degree programs are not held accountable by the federal government for job training toward gainful employment, ask the provost about removing programs such as engineering and teaching. And ask the marketing department about pulling advertising that ties enrollment to career achievement. It is about both, but faculty needs to embrace job training and students, education enrichment, an incongruousness of traditional higher education.

In 2011, the Obama Administration removed the twelve safe harbors related to the Higher Education Act's (HEA) incentive compensation clause. Was gainful employment needed since eliminating the safe harbors had the desired impact of slowing down the career education sector and deafening interest from Wall Street?

If the gainful employment manifesto delivers as intended, community colleges will be overwhelmed without the benefit of adequate state dollars, never mind nonexistent endowments or forbidden investor capital. That equates to inordinate amounts of wasted federal Pell Grants, frustrated students, and stressed-out instructors. Proposed free tuition initiatives will intensify the anticipated overcrowding.

More for-profit colleges might fail the 90/10 rule if including veterans' tuition benefits in the formula. It might be fascinating to see an analysis of how many tuition-dependent nonprofit colleges exceed ninety percent of revenue from Title IV funds. When including veterans' benefits, how many exceed ninety percent? For the most part, this information is unavailable to anyone beyond the administrations and boards of trustees of these politically protected, non-tax generating secret societies.

Since the rules forbid for-profit institutions from having an endowment, take it further and calculate 90/10 for nonprofits, sans any funding generated revenue. It may never happen, although it should because when it comes to taxpayer dollars, citizens deserve full disclosure without built-in protection for Title IV institutions based on tax status.

On Profit Versus Nonprofit in Higher Education

It is a naïve value system that believes nonprofit means good and for-profit means bad. Another reminder of my father's creed, "Whether for-profit or nonprofit, remember it is about the money."

That for-profit postsecondary education exists should be an embarrassment to the state-owned public and private nonprofit sectors.

Virtually every member of Congress, staffers at the U.S. Department of Education, and journalists and editors in the mainstream media are alums of traditional higher education institutions. The bias is built in at the starting gate.

When students fail or debt up at for-profits, it is often deemed the school or company's doing. On the contrary, when students fail or debt up at traditional public and nonprofits, it is not uncommon to be judged as the student's responsibility. Such an opposing dynamic is the result of conflicting business models. At a for-profit, the student is a paying customer to be taught and served by faculty and staff. At the traditional public or nonprofit, a student is an invited guest—albeit a paying one—of the faculty, administration, coaches, and researchers. Community colleges are somewhere in between these two paradigms.

Not for profit translates to no taxes are paid on profit or surplus. What if we taxed property, equipment, big-time athletics, and capital gains from endowments, then earmarked the increased government revenue for additional Pell grants as well as improving community colleges and other non-elite state schools? Nonprofits are required to tax payroll. Perhaps the faculty and staff need the money more than the million-dollar Wall Street endowment managers and elite athletic coaches. Why tax the payroll, but not property, equipment, athletics, or capital gains?

When pondering the myriad of for-profit vendors that serve state-owned and private nonprofit colleges and universities, including the academic departments, one comprehends a significant amount of non-profit institutional revenues are landing in the hands of shareholders as potential profits earned; an inconvenient truth of the higher education industrial complex.

Faculty, staff, and administrators at career education colleges where I worked were there to make a difference in students' lives. The personal war stories heard from students were cringe-worthy. To help resurrect or reinvent lives through practical postsecondary education, virtually one at a time, is a noble mission. I understand a nonprofit may construe this approach as lowering academic standards. At a for-profit, it is called helping to build a life that nobody else took an interest in.

High school teachers and guidance counselors have been telling students for years, "Do as I did and go to a traditional four-year college and then to grad school." When attempting to promote my career college, high school staff members sometimes countered with pronouncements such as, "Ninety-eight percent of our students go to traditional colleges."

My response was, "Then may I speak with the two percent that is not?" Only to find the two percent was twenty percent when considering alternative student plans for military enlistment, direct to work, time off, or yikes, attending a for-profit training school. Or sixty-eight percent if you count how many, on average, will attend and then withdraw from traditional four-year colleges that combined graduate only about thirty-two percent of the general adult population nationwide. That is a long way from ninety-eight percent.

Please send high school students to where each has the best chance to be successful, whether at a traditional, community, or vocational college; the military; peace corps or equivalent; the workplace; a year on the road; or volunteering for church, temple, mosque, or charity. Focus on what will work for that individual student instead of what worked for the teacher, guidance counselor, or journalist. When gauging how college completion rates and job prospects are out of sync with acquired tuition debt and exhausted taxpayer subsidies, this everyone goes to a four-year traditional college thing, since the late 1980's, is failing us.

Based on direct experience, I can accept traditional higher education's attack on for-profit degree-granting colleges and universities. When fighting counter-lobbies during expansions into degree-granting, nursing programs, and other startups typical to the traditional model, I was reminded that some loathe the competition.

I witnessed an elected state legislator say during a public meeting, "We trust a nonprofit, unequivocally, to do as it sees fit."

I stopped hiring former traditional college faculty and staff long ago, despite the propensity for impressive academic credentials and publications presented on their curriculum vitae. In general, most struggled to comprehend—or refused to embrace—the concept of student-centric teaching and learning that is standard to the career education sector.

Move toward the awarding of credentials at completion levels throughout two and four-year degree programs. Under this format, students now considered as dropped are classified as completed. Employers then make hiring decisions based on job descriptions requiring varying levels of course completion.

One thing traditional colleges, in general, can learn from the for-profits: select a commencement keynote speaker for the benefit of the students, as opposed to the board of trustees or the office of public information and its media contacts. Plus, have the faculty, staff, and administration take more of a backseat in celebration of the graduating students and families.

Suggested content of a proposed letter addressed to the president of the University of Michigan, with copies to Michigan governor and U.S. secretary of education: asking why it is acceptable to the university, and the state, to pay its new head football coach one and a half times what ECMC paid for fifty-six Corinthian College campuses. Reportedly, Coach Jim Harbaugh will be paid $35 million over seven years. His assignment is to serve 105 Wolverines. In contrast, ECMC, a nonprofit, spent a total of $24 million to acquire Corinthian Colleges—a bankrupt for-profit—and the federal government to save 39,000 Corinthian students. The math equates to $47,500 per Michigan football player each season versus $600 per Corinthian student. No place as higher education to muddle one's priorities.

Faculty and staff that taught and served at the career schools, colleges, and companies I worked for throughout my career had an innate ability to motivate challenged students to step up, believe in themselves, and work as a team, similar to a successful football coach. A stark difference and the sad truth are each was paid the full-time equivalent of about $50,000 per year for the effort, not $5 million.

I have observed tolerance for individuals making enormous amounts of money from nonprofit or state-owned institutions, whereas there is less support for making money at profit-seeking organizations. Being for-profit organizations are comprised of people as well; it is a curious distinction.

Postsecondary education is just that, postsecondary education, and it should be regulated, legislated, and judged as one. Share the same regulatory footing regardless of capital sources, ownership, or tax status, whether exempt or contributor. The responsibility then remains with the institution and its stakeholders to position itself as competitive or non-competitive in admissions; research or learning-based; faculty or student-centered; regional or national accredited; school, college, or university status; Title IV or cash; interscholastic or intramural athletics; on-ground or online delivery; traditional, vocational, or competency learning; and so forth. Accreditors, legislators, and regulators, then assure quality and access in the public interest. In other words, integrate the present model of divergent platforms—public, nonprofit, and proprietary—founded on bias and elitism.

It is time to stop separating based on tax status and treat all higher education institutions as one industry. And yes, it is an industry, a money-making machine. The difference being that two classifications, public and nonprofit, have the general support of elected politicians and the mainstream media, and the other, proprietary or for-profit, do not. Judge each institution by its merits. Borrowing an investment anecdote attributed to Warren Buffett, "When the tide goes out, we will see who is swimming naked."

Divide and conquer are meant for war, assuming war is necessary. It has no place in higher education.

And the move to nonprofit status by several career education sector companies is fascinating, driven by onerous regulations and misguided stigma. This annexation from the for-profit education sector mirrors recent changes in domicile location by some U.S. multinational corporations to avoid higher domestic income tax burdens. My sense is federal and state governments, the education companies that converted to nonprofit, and expatriate corporations, will come to regret this paradigm of regulation and tax avoidance because there is no better place than the United States of America to live, learn and earn.

It appears most traditional four-year institutions remain committed to being selective in the admission of students. And that is to be respected as long as each observes the nondiscriminatory statements printed in its catalog.

If recent reports are accurate that traditional four-year enrollments are up slightly, and community college and career education sector enrollments are down considerably, are significant numbers of community college and career education sector targeted students thereby attending nowhere? If so, the pundits, at least on a subconscious level, are getting what was wanted. Affluent and smart ones continue to attend college as the poor and academically challenged settle for minimum wage jobs, boots on the ground, the local hangout, online gaming, or incarceration.

Why are aggressive attempts at meeting enrollment goals at nonprofits deemed a necessary evil, yet at for-profits, just evil?

Quality academic and training programs triumph in the end.

On the Stigma of For-Profit Career Education

Many good thespians in for-profit career education are often portrayed as a troupe of bad actors.

The sector has perceived worse outcomes and higher reliance on government money because of open enrollment that caters to the non-traditional, first-generation college students that traditional four-year institutions ignore, reject, or fail. Community colleges attract a similar student to the for-profit.

Selective admission keeps out the poor and huddled masses. Both community and career sector colleges are endeared to welcome—faculty at both might say, "Happy to welcome"—the student who wants to be somebody despite being told since birth they are a nobody. Perhaps it is time for the higher education industrial complex to stop penalizing the community colleges and for-profits for valiant attempts to serve this ever-growing student population in America. These students deserve a chance, not a judgment.

As a rule, open enrollment institutions have lower graduation and higher default rates. Public discourse is rare regarding open enrollment students who graduate, get jobs, and pay back student loans. Why not count successful career education sector students as well? There appears a pervasive culture of focusing on successful students from one category of the institution and unsuccessful students from another.

Unfortunately, the sector has failed to counter the negative publicity with the abundance of positive outcomes its institutions provide to the economy and the community — a conspicuous shortcoming of the sector's efforts during the Obama administration.

Suppose skeptical observers devoted just one week to visiting reputable for-profit institutions. I guarantee most are surprised how different, ethical, and productive the sector is from stereotypes generated by the bad players that dominate the media.

Public acknowledgment of the dedicated, ethical, and hardworking faculty and staff, as well as successful students at for-profit career education schools, colleges, and universities, is rare in this debate. Guilt by unintended association does not define a professional. Suppose I were an outsider who happened upon regular college education assessments by mainstream media, government, or traditional education. In that case,

I might postulate every employee as a crook and every student as hood-winked into failure. But those innuendos are far from the truth.

Some critics of the for-profit sector refuse to believe successful students exist, thereby writing off positive stories as false and negative stories as true. Indeed, a head-scratcher.

I have witnessed opponents portray career education students as desperate. Why is being desperate for education such a bad thing? My grandparents were desperate when coming to America with an equivalent eighth-grade level education; worked desperately to give their children at least high school level educations; and in turn, were desperate to influence their grandchildren to pursue a college education using any gifts, savings, grants, scholarships, or loans available. I am forever grateful for this generational desperation for career training.

A majority of students attending career education schools where I served were shrewd consumers. Some shopped other career schools and the community college, asked about accreditation, faculty credentials, equipment, and employment opportunities. Akin to typical big-ticket item consumers, they understood the price tag but focused on month-to-month affordability. These hardworking, motivated students more often come from lower-income, first-generation college families. Despite this, some observers in the media, think tanks, and government, depict many as ignorant victims.

I witnessed a poignant speech given by the former commissioner of a regional accreditor at his retirement dinner. At one point, he acknowledged the for-profit school employees in the audience, reminiscing how his father, a first-generation American, learned a career skill at a for-profit school. The training and subsequent career allowed his father to put the commissioner through an Ivy League university, and in turn, his children through elite private nonprofit colleges as well. The commissioner implied that without attending the career school, its different tax status notwithstanding, his father may have missed an opportunity to pursue the American Dream. There is perhaps a lesson here. Respect the career education student. One day, they might send their children to your elite institution, serve as a regional accreditation commissioner, or employ you.

It appears, in general, that anti-for-profit education articles and posts focus on the corporate suite and Wall Street, ignoring the education institutions filled with earnest students, dedicated faculty and staff, and ethical administrators.

At the time of this writing, and despite presumed hardship at the starting gate, seventy-eight percent of students in the career education sector—from the most recent federal three-year cohort rate—were not in default on student loans. Why does the anti-for-profit agenda ignore the successful majority?

A prominent U.S. senator, a Democrat, visited a career school campus that I led. As part of his proposed agenda, he planned to meet with several students for a roundtable discussion. As any postsecondary institution, we picked model students. However, the dean, department chairs, and instructors courtesy prepped each for the meeting as we were not aware of what specific questions the senator planned to ask the students.

He asked just one question, "Why did you choose this career school over the local community college that costs one-third the tuition?" The students, aware each was paying more, proceeded to explain to the senator why they were more satisfied with the career school than the community or state colleges previously attended by them or a family member, without achieving the desired outcome of graduating and securing dignified employment. I was pinching myself as the senator expressed his pleasure with the enthusiastic answers to his frank question. He was perhaps a bit surprised, but I had the privilege of knowing how committed the faculty and staff were to our students' success and well-being.

Cosmetology schools stood out on a list of heightened scrutiny released by the U.S. Department of Education. But in its minimal format, the list neglected to explain that beauty and barber schools teach programs that state health departments regulate. These regulations often require curricula of between 1,200 and 1,800 hours for the student to sit for the required licensing exams, both written and practical. Such understandable rigor requires capital-intensive investment, the recruitment of experienced practitioners as instructors who are further schooled and licensed to teach the courses, plus large doses of learning product consumed each day. Arduous monitoring, to remain in compliance with state regulations, also requires significant expense. Therefore, tuition runs as high as $20,000 per program.

An observer might be compelled to ask, "What if we taught these beauty programs at low-cost community colleges?" See capital-intensive investment. "Why not encourage students to attend the alternative vocational technical high school for free?" That is where the stigma comes in. Contrary to conventional wisdom—as discovered in my direct experience as executive director of a national brand name cosmetology school—the students are the brightest, most creative, and passionate in postsecondary education. Despite this commitment, as children, many are deterred by parents, teachers, counselors, and mainstream media from pursuing their chosen vocation. Later, as an adult, after failing at the traditional college where there was little interest in attending, to begin with, does the student pursue their dream as a licensed beauty or barbering professional.

It is important to remember, similar to community colleges, career education sector schools, colleges, and universities have open or less competitive admissions policies. It is irrational to ask each to live up to traditional colleges' standards, including competitive entry requirements and legacies of attracting students blessed with superior affluence and intellect.

Two misnomers about for-profit colleges that I often observe in the media, including reader comments, are 1) grade inflation is rampant, and 2) students are better off at community colleges and other lower-cost nonprofit trade schools if made aware of the option. My counter is 1) accusations of grade inflation occur at elite universities as well, including professors being pressured by influential donor parents; and

2) significant numbers of career education students had dropped from community colleges or state four-year schools and are well aware of the difference in tuition.

When crafting headlines, why do some editors in the mainstream media use only the alleged nonprofit bad actor's institutional name in the caption yet signify the career education suspected bad actor as a for-profit?

On Accreditation

National accreditors have prescriptive standards focused on student outcomes. I have served on regional and national accreditation visit teams and was a recipient of regional and national team visits. As a school operator, given a choice, I prefer being reviewed by the peer-only regional team. To simplify, as long as the institution is strong financially, meets the rigorous criteria for faculty credentials, has a documented learning assessment program, is governed by an independent board, and is the Americans with Disabilities Act (ADA) accessible, it is good to go for another ten years.

On the other hand, for a national team visit—often including an accreditation staff member's physical presence to monitor for any shenanigans by the peer group—the institution needs to be operating on all cylinders, especially when assessing student outcomes. If not, the consequences may include facing several months of writing a detailed response, a year of burdensome reporting requirements, or worse, a show-cause directive asking the institution to defend its accreditation worthiness.

As part of a national accreditation visit team, I spent hours calling employers to verify institutional reported graduate job placement numbers. When I volunteered to verify graduate employment on a regional accreditation visit team, I was instructed by the team chair, "Do not bother; it is not in the standards."

To be sure, regional accreditation is challenging to obtain from the outset. But once in the club, it is relatively easy to stay, especially for a private nonprofit. In my observations, regional accreditors seem more rigid on the state-owned publics, and of course, on the for-profits. Arguably, national accreditation is easier to obtain at first, although when up for reaffirmation, do not take the national team for granted, or else.

Programmatic accreditation, perhaps the most challenging form of accreditation to obtain and maintain, in general, is a credible platform for demonstrating program quality to students, employers, and the community as a whole. For-profit education would strengthen its public image if it embraced programmatic accreditation as part of a sector-wide commitment to the pursuit of quality.

On the Student Loan Debt Crisis

If for-profits and community colleges encompass fifty percent of the student loan cohort defaults, then state-owned public and private non-profits combine for the other half of defaults. Selective traditional colleges and universities screen and cherry-pick students upfront. There is no excuse for sharing half of student loan defaults.

Take career education sector and community colleges out of the student loan debt crisis discussion as the odds are stacked against both based on open enrollment to high-risk students.

The proverb: *the one who holds the gold makes the rules*, again applies. As long as higher education institutions rely on taxpayer support for survival, i.e., community colleges, state colleges and universities, tuition-dependent nonprofits, and for-profit career education, then the federal government's Title IV program will prevail and continue to dictate policy. The alternative is each state introducing its comprehensive student loan program, although improbable beyond the rhetoric of those committed to state-centric interpretations of the constitution. In contrast, private nonprofit universities are susceptible to the influence of donors who fund the endowment.

I suggest the awarding of financial aid be taken away from the schools and be dispersed by private federal contractors at convenient physical locations and online. The student's individual award is transmitted to the approved, accredited school, college, or university of their choice. It sounds similar to the voucher programs that have failed to take hold in primary and secondary education. However, local school districts are a different breed when considering the politics involved. In postsecondary education, you are dealing with adults using a federal entitlement program that requires payback in most situations, as student loans far exceed Pell grants.

And no disrespect to the thousands of dedicated financial aid professionals as the hypothetical local and regional service centers create an abundance of job opportunities. Let the feds and students take responsibility for awarding and dispersing the tuition funding, thus allowing accredited schools, colleges, and universities admitting the qualified students to focus on ethical admission, quality education, engaged student services, and successful career placement.

Until then, the lender, i.e., the U.S. Department of Education; the broker, i.e., the Title IV authorized institution; and the borrower, i.e., the student plus any cosigners, are each accountable for the joint participation.

* * *

Fifty-four years later, and despite Eisenhower's forewarning, the military-industrial complex is as powerful as ever. Will the dynamics of the higher education industrial complex continue unabated as well? Do the privileged that pulled the long straw at birth continue to benefit from higher education at the expense of those citizens unwillingly holding the short straw, and at what additional cost to taxpayers and the economy?

Nine

A RENEWED VALUE PROPOSITION FOR POSTSECONDARY CAREER EDUCATION

THE PAIN OF CHANGE IS LONG FORGOTTEN WHEN THE BENEFITS OF THE CHANGE ARE REALIZED.

In the 1970s, John Sperling, founder of Apollo Education Group, pioneered an unprecedented growth of the for-profit education sector in the United States from a sleepy group of privately owned trade schools to the behemoth publicly traded and private equity-owned operators of today. Apollo offered a then profound value proposition to the proliferation of working adult students: an alternative learning environment to the predominance of post-high school, youthful, traditional colleges and universities of the time.

Sperling's novel higher education model became a hit, and just as hit songs get mimicked in the music industry, hit business models get replicated on Wall Street and Main Street. Established operators soon jumped on the bandwagon. Startups flourished in the wake. In 1991, DeVry Education Group one-upped Apollo Education by becoming the first publicly traded U.S. education provider, soon followed by initial public offerings from both Apollo and ITT Educational Services in 1994.

Today, several publicly traded career education companies remain. Over three thousand privately held U.S. companies are deriving primary revenues from postsecondary educational services. After the sector's peak in 2010, high student default rates, a weak job market, accreditation issues, negative media coverage, and removal of the twelve safe harbors led to lower enrollment, falling profits, plummeting stock prices, and campus closures.

Finding a niche or unique competitive advantage is again the developing story in a sector at or near its bottom. Value propositions have become a driving force toward reinvention. Companies and campuses that lead the way will remain viable and improve public images. But to renew competitiveness and value toward noteworthy contributions to twenty-first century workforce development, more needs to be done.

Consider Japan's TQM as a Rekindled Value Proposition

In the global economy that emerged following World War II, products manufactured and exported by Japanese multinational companies were considered by many Americans as cheap, low-quality imitations. Granted, a post-World War II prejudice toward the Japanese played into those perceptions, yet a resurgence of the Japanese business culture emerged. The response from Japan was engineered by American statistician W. Edwards Deming, among others, and became known as total quality management or TQM.

Beginning in the late 1960s to early 1970s, led by companies such as Toyota and Sony, Japan's subsequent shift toward quality control and customer satisfaction reversed the previous negative view. The Japanese multinationals flourished by filling the void in quality ignored by American producers. Ironic was that Japan's resurgence occurred not long before Apollo Education Group introduced its adult learner model.

Akin to the reinvigorated Japanese manufacturers in the last half of the twentieth century, the career education sector is expected to survive and prosper in this century's new global economy. As long as government-subsidized programs—targeted at community and other public colleges—continue to fall short in building and maintaining America's workforce development infrastructure, market forces will call on the career education sector to fill training gaps.

But who among the education service providers will emerge as the sector's Toyota or Sony, improving the poor quality, low return perception of for-profit education in the U.S.? Companies and institutions that figure this out now will benefit in a way that would make John Sperling and other industry founders proud of the timely and triumphant renewal of a universal value proposition for U.S. for-profit postsecondary education.

Defeat Gainful Employment with Excellent Outcomes

Career education companies and institutions will be forced to overcome the current regulatory and elitist onslaught by delivering academic learning, career training, and student services better than their non-profit counterparts. Achieve gainful employment metrics by way of affordable tuition and employer partnerships. And remember to monitor default management for the gainfully employed and non-graduates as well. Granted, federal judges and legislators sidestepped the sector this time, although universal quality outcomes will silence even the harshest of critics.

Commencing July 1, 2015, the U.S. Department of Education's goal with gainful employment was to link graduates' jobs and income to a career school's continued eligibility in administering Title IV federal aid in approved programs of study. When Main Street returns to an economic boom cycle, higher-cost degree programs' inherent financial risk may lessen, although this event remains elusive considering today's stagnant economic climate.

Continued slow growth on Main Street could mitigate further congressional action in response to gainful employment and the student loan crisis. Regardless of economic conditions, gainful employment will temper any penchant for raising tuition in the for-profit sector.

Renew Employer Partnerships

The career college where I served as assistant director of admissions enjoyed a generous scholarship program with a major bank in Manhattan. The bank offered several full scholarships to incoming students in an executive assistant program. A caveat was if hired by the bank upon graduation, an award recipient had to commit to two years of full-time employment. Another stipulation was an expectation that the career college sends to the bank the best candidates available from each graduating cycle.

Today, similar employer partnerships remain across the sector yet appear more exception than the rule.

Veterans of the career training sector know that significant numbers of entry-level jobs filled with graduates of career sector programs were once recruited and trained by the employer at its sole expense. Today, the cost of training is paid by the career education student. Employers, the sector's ultimate stakeholder, have had it good under this third-party formal training paradigm. On the whole, employers have saved enormous training expenses by recruiting the sector's graduates. But the survival of the sector will depend on a compromise of shared capital from the employer and private sector school, college, or university. In other words, swing the pendulum to a more equitable alliance.

To guarantee targeted success levels, the school, student, and employer must contribute some skin to the partnership. Employer-sponsored equipment, internships, and scholarships, supplemented by lower tuition from the institution, may suffice. And students can be screened in advance for specific career program merit, based on employer guidelines. These and similar alliances are potential game-changers.

Facilitate Returns on Student Tuition Investment

Regardless of employer participation, the student's ability to graduate and secure gainful employment remains vital to paying back student loans used to finance the education.

My general rule of thumb is to limit total student tuition commitment to the average potential first-year income of the chosen field of study. This first-year salary rule assumes the student is relying on a career for primary income instead of an affluent household or trust fund. Granted, privileged students will survive the student loan debt crisis.

There is substantial evidence that, on average, workers with earned degrees surpass those with no degrees in salary over the long term. But the one to one tuition to wage rule takes advantage of shorter-term return opportunities during the critical time frame when student loans first enter payback, the period when defaults are most susceptible. Nonetheless, the risk/reward proposition appears to favor reward in shorter, less expensive career training, whereas risk escalates with longer, higher-cost programs.

As of this writing, the above rule of thumb is not a regulatory requirement but based on experience and observations. Nevertheless, the U.S. Department of Education appears committed—by its gainful employment guidelines—to regulate the return on tuition investment for career education students, as measured by loan to income ratios.

Be Wonderful by Embracing Regulations

Another favorite verse of wisdom widely credited to the billionaire investor, Warren Buffett:

" *I try to buy stock in businesses that are so wonderful that an idiot can run them. Because sooner or later one will.* "

Insiders responsible for destroying the reputation of long-standing, value-added, for-profit U.S. postsecondary education are either already gone from the sector or will be in time as the overdue shakeup continues. Underestimating the substantial stake of federal and state governments in education company operations led to the sector-wide fall from grace.

Focusing on the current Wall Street quarter, over-aggressive lobbying, and voting on party lines were failed attempts at equitable solutions. Playing by the rules and treating the students, graduates, employers, and taxpayers with reverence were never off the table. First, being an outstanding provider to these primary stakeholders will deliver adequate rewards to beneficiary stakeholders such as owners and employees. In hindsight, the reversal of this pecking order enriched some in the short term, at the expense of many in the long run. As a consequence, the proverbial fan suffered a direct hit.

In response to the slowdown in student enrollment, company executives pointed to broader economic concerns. But economics are often driven by business cycles and thus carried little weight in the blame game. The fall-off was inevitable following the countercyclical record run-up in enrollment growth during the Great Recession of 2008-2010. Regardless, the removal of the twelve safe harbors by the Obama administration brought the growth spurt to a grinding halt. Unable to motivate the sales team without risking sanctions to award federal financial aid to its customers put the sector in defense mode. Today, career education companies remain on that side of the ball.

In retrospect, regulatory compliance and responsible student services are immune to business cycles. The lesson being stakeholders must respect this exposure when calculating the intrinsic value of education companies. And the companies need to make clean regulatory records an integral part of the value proposition.

Quality academics, engaging student services, and high graduate employment are now vital components of a typical company's strategic plan. That is the simple part. Producing strong regulatory and accreditation records with consistency will benefit students, employers, taxpayers, and shareholders alike. Not doing or remaining so will lead to an education company's peril, regardless of any attractive metrics.

And the steadfast commitment of the U.S. Department of Education's gainful employment regulations is a reminder to career education companies and their stakeholders that headwinds remain in the windshield, not the rearview mirror. Although ignoring the vital role of the sector in America's workforce development of the twenty-first century because of a blanketed perception of regulatory risk could squander outstanding investment, employment, and learning opportunities.

Blow the Bubble on Student Loan Debt Crisis

Following years of public scrutiny directed, for the most part, at for-profit, postsecondary institutions, the ever-expanding student loan debt crisis is now bringing all U.S. higher education into its growing bubble.

As widely reported, the number of student loans awarded in 2013 crossed $100 billion for the first time. Total outstanding loans exceeded an unprecedented $1 trillion in 2014. Americans owed more on student loans than credit cards.

First enacted by Congress in 1965, The Higher Education Act (HEA) was last reauthorized in 2008 as the Higher Education Opportunity Act. It includes the programs under Title IV that are the primary source of federal student financial aid. The United States Department of Education secretary is responsible for administering the regulations on behalf of the federal government's executive branch.

In advance of the next reauthorization of the HEA, scheduled for late 2015, Congress is mulling both the lowering of interest rates on student loans as well as implementing an automatic income-based repayment program. With past-due student loan payments at an all-time high, it is evident that federal action is warranted. Because of objective eligibility requirements, unintended disparities between student loan awards and job income prospects occur regularly across higher education. Members of Congress and student loan reformers advocating the automatic income-based repayment plan are perhaps aware of the existing voluntary program that allows eligible students to pay back loans at fifteen percent of discretionary income.

Opposing opinions may demand students are mindful of the fact that an automatic plan already exists. However, it appears revamping the student loan program by forcing borrowers into a structured income-based repayment does not go far enough. A delinquent payer's challenge will persist if the student has borrowed an amount that does not compliment the chosen career's income potential. If not corrected, observers may further examine the student financing process's front end and recommend new methodologies to control the amounts allocated in loan awards, including applying gainful employment to every Title IV authorized institution of higher learning.

The student loan debt crisis encompasses the whole of the higher education industrial complex. Participants in this quandary include benefactors of traditional public, private nonprofit, and private for-profit institutions such as senior executives, administrators, faculty, staff, high net worth donors, investors, notable alumni, athletic boosters, mainstream media, and elected politicians.

Of late, some elite members of the higher education industrial complex targeted the student loan crisis as rooted in the now vilified for-profit education sector. Mind you, not an orchestrated conspiracy, but self-interest protection of the tax-exempt adherents of the complex. Nonetheless, it came at the expense of the tax-generating, vulnerable for-profit sector and its blindsided stakeholders.

Whether attending a public, nonprofit, or for-profit college, it is the taxpayer that remains accountable for having invested in a student who failed to follow through as intended, i.e., to graduate, secure a job, or transfer to a higher level of learning, thus contributing to society in a meaningful way. It is undeniable that career education institutions are over-reliant on government grants and student loans. But I challenge any reader to look beyond the for-profits and question the supporting roles of state-owned public and private nonprofits in the potential abuse of taxpayer subsidies.

There are significant numbers of tuition-driven public and private nonprofit colleges and universities that might perish without state or local taxpayer subsidies and federal student loans or grants. And except for payroll taxes and voluntary contributions to local police and fire departments serving its campuses, not much else is returned to the tax coffers by traditional institutions.

Consequently, it is too narrow a focus to limit the student loan discussion to for-profits when all higher education, sans the heavily endowed institutions, is in a proverbial bubble bursting at the seams. But the sector can make a difference and lead the way in orchestrating controllable student loan management systems. It is an inherited obligation and an opportunity to generate a renewed respect for the sector.

Chase Student Demand with Differentiation

Become the lower cost, quality operator by reducing general sales and admin on the income statement, i.e., marketing, admissions, financial aid, campus administration, and corporate overhead; and raising the percentage of revenue invested in education services and facilities, i.e., instructional costs, student services, career services, and physical over-head.

Career education companies can increase education services expenditures closer to fifty percent of revenue and decrease general sales and admin nearer to thirty percent, thus yielding an operating margin in the neighborhood of twenty percent. Holistic financial models provide an opportunity to satisfy the primary constituents of students, regulators, and shareholders. Historically, the sector has struggled with a balance benefiting all stakeholders.

One sure way to decrease administrative costs is by reducing bad debt. Lower bad debt reflects the stable combination of satisfied students and effective collection strategies, including the administrative capability of processing Title IV financial aid. And keeping tuition costs reasonable will be paramount for success from the expected narrower product mix of the gainful employment era.

It appears the new normal will be quality, low-cost companies, and institutions, boasting believable business models with a firm grasp on how to leverage competitive advantages in a hybrid world of on-ground and online education delivery.

Develop Twenty-First Century Enrollment Models

Successful career education graduates or completers that refuse to refer new students offer the explanation, "Great school, but too expensive." It is a perceived value issue. I have witnessed this phenomenon in my campus's student and graduate survey results with feedback equating to: "Wonderful instructors; beneficial program; caring staff; clean, modern building; and I love my job. But the cost of attendance was too expensive."

As discussed in chapter five, Playing the Game the Right Way, a logical move for the sector is quality education and student services delivered at a reasonable cost that produces legacy enrollments, thus lessening the need to buy new students with ubiquitous online web initiatives. A potential solution to unraveling the sector's conflicted image as overpriced, regardless of successful outcomes, is producing a majority of new enrollments from referrals by combining quality, affordable education with relevant social media platforms.

Raise the Bar for Accreditation and Community Relations

Hold regional accreditation as exclusive to degree-granting institutions, thereby lessening the debacle in the transfer of credit. Reserve national accreditation for diploma or certificate level schools to take advantage of its high prescriptive standards for student outcomes.

When lobbying government officials, stakeholders in the career education sector need to avoid exclusive political party affiliations in the workplace and instead brag about excellent student and institutional outcomes to both sides of the legislative aisle.

Campus presidents of for-profit schools, colleges, and universities need to be out in the local community as active members of the chamber of commerce, visiting employers, lobbying elected officials, and supporting relevant charities. The presence of capable department directors and permissive ownership or senior management is imperative in allowing campus leaders to develop a productive public image. By unintentional design, school leaders onboarded as mere plant managers will neglect the positive impact of community relations.

The House's former Speaker, the late Tip O'Neill, suggested, "All politics are local." Get out of your office and join traditional college education leaders in the community and at the state capital. Show elected officials, regulators, employers, the media, and other influential locals how your career education institution, through workforce development, impacts their constituents' socioeconomic ascension. And then back up your pledge by extending personal invitations to visit your campus or company.

Confront the New Disruption in Online Education

U.S. career education companies offering online programs face a new disruption, not called gainful employment; President Obama's college public disclosure initiative; or the Senate Health, Education, Labor, and Pensions Committee (HELP.) A burgeoning threat is the onslaught of online offerings from the nation's traditional nonprofit colleges and universities. In an ironic twist, some of these institutions—both public and private—are flexing marketing muscle similar to the for-profits, with an aggressive approach sometimes condemned by the traditional schools themselves.

Nonprofits are emerging as the principal threat to U.S. career sector online education companies, using a for-profit archetype paradigm of aggressive marketing, student-centered business models, and in some instances, less competitive admission standards. Organized faculty, the cultural center of nonprofit institutions, are, in some cases, expressing dismay with these determined online efforts.

An insider at a prominent nonprofit online university shared with me the for-profit model of aggressive marketing is in play and supported by traditional college administrations and boards of trustees, any faculty malcontent notwithstanding. But tuition-dependent nonprofits, lacking their elite brethren's substantial endowments, are building sizable endowments from online program surplus. A universal term of nonprofit organizations, surplus translates to profits at the tax-exempt institutions. Internal redistribution of excess dollars is targeted for new buildings and scholarship programs, akin to investment from capital markets at postsecondary career education operators that allocate those funds for similar infrastructure improvements.

The notable difference is that for-profit education institutions generate local, state, and federal income and property taxes due to continuing operations. In contrast, direct contributions to state and federal tax revenues from tuition-dependent nonprofit institutions are limited to mere payroll deductions.

Owners or investors may observe this long-disputed disparity in allocating revenue and generating taxes is beginning to dwindle outside of biased mainstream media, interested public servants, and other anti-for-profit ideologues. For example, President Obama's proposed, albeit watered down, accountability program for traditional colleges and universities using federal financial aid is a sign that nonprofits are no longer exempt from arbitrary government scrutiny, thus providing for-profit educators the renewed prospect of competing on a more level playing field.

To regain footing on this coveted ground of opportunity in hybrid learning, career education companies will need to show consistency with believable value propositions, competitive tuition rates, quality academics, and robust regulatory compliance. The challenge is reversing the renewed threat from nonprofit online operators by meeting those institutions on the alleged lower cost, higher quality academic platforms.

Progressive transformation in cost and quality could give the for-profits a unique opportunity to outshine within the early twenty-first century's emerging higher education reinvention. According to a recent survey by Northeastern University, just forty-one percent of Americans believe online education provides similar quality to traditional on-ground models. Online operators may need to address this universal perception issue in a rare collaboration.

For the career sector, parity may be achieved by increasing public disclosure of the substantial tax revenues already contributed by the for-profits to surrounding communities and the nation. The sector's significant returns to the tax base are in stark contrast to the high-cost elite residual programs from the tax-exempt educational institutions, such as competitive athletics, to the benefit of a privileged few.

Whether a student, taxpayer, investor, or donor, higher education is an investment-worthy of returns to all constituents, but only if expected outcomes contribute to noteworthy socioeconomic development. Frankly, an institution of higher learning's tax status does not determine its core value to society.

The best online schools will win by serving targeted populations with quality education and student services, irrespective of Internal Revenue Service designations. Whether investing in a for-profit education company's equity, donating to a nonprofit alma mater's endowment, or paying a loved one's college tuition, albeit profit or nonprofit, caveat emptor prevails. It appears a sincere commitment to delivering high-quality education at reasonable tuition cost, something the sector has struggled with for years leading up to its notorious dusting by the Obama administration.

The ensuing onslaught of federal and state government agencies resulted from the sector's steady annual tuition hikes, i.e., higher costs for students, decoupled by reductions in instructional spending, i.e., lower costs for owners, leading to the current road to near ruin. Often cited as primary sources of failure are excessive government intervention and regulatory pressures. Although a commitment to building a legacy reputation via a counter-intuitive, low tuition cost, high-quality education model—often resisted by the sector—remains a plausible solution.

Opportunity Beckons the Career Education Sector

As the for-profit education sector mends its well-publicized woes, it will be critical to lobby that all higher learning institutions be held accountable to students and the taxpayers who fund these partnerships — a universal expectation of generating returns on investment from genuine career opportunities that justify tuition paid.

But the career education sector must set the example, together or in a continued shakeout. If this occurs, the sector's stakeholders will benefit from a resumption of consistent growth and profitability, albeit reinforced by quality academic delivery and strong regulatory compliance. Until then, the sector appears to remain in limbo pending further consequences of the student loan debt crisis and early results from the gainful employment ruling directed indiscriminately toward it.

During a down business cycle, senior management at for-profit education companies were awarded, as corporate staffers and employees at the campus level were laid off or squeezed into expanded roles, with minimal or no additional compensation. But this behavior is not exclusive to the career education sector. It has become the dominant American business model, or bubble, that will correct itself with forced regulations or natural economic cycles, provoking a welcomed narrowing of the income gap.

Forever standing at the center of the regulatory radar, career education may bask in a rare positive light by contributing its counter to this Main Street sensitive controversy of pay disparity, long before other sectors covered by Wall Street or the national media. The average lower socioeconomic status of its students before enrollment dictates the sector takes the lead on this front-page issue.

I believe the vast majority of postsecondary career education workers are caring, student-centered, and passionate about educating disadvantaged Americans for skilled jobs. The sector's professionals are committed to providing students an opportunity to improve their socioeconomic standing. This genuine stakeholder devotion is refreshing in today's apathetic, low service consumer environment; a compelling reason to expect long-term survival for the sector, bad actors, notwithstanding.

It is plausible the sector's burgeoning third act will revert to its historical first act of shorter-term, on-ground, vocational-based training. Students complete these programs at the associate's degree, diploma, or certificate level, thereby affording lower total tuition costs than training at higher degree levels. Nevertheless, online adult learning is expected to survive with significant growth ahead.

But shorter-term training may become a necessary paradigm shift within U.S. postsecondary education, as both for-profit and nonprofit operators are beginning to crowd the online and advanced degree markets. Entry-level students find hands-on career training programs such as skilled trades, culinary, cosmetology, information technology support, graphic design, and allied health difficult to master in a one hundred percent online environment. And bachelor's degrees, or higher, are seldom necessary for employment success from this program mix.

Based on U.S. Census Bureau data, by the year 2012, close to fifty percent of Americans, age twenty-five or older, had achieved more than a high school diploma, although less than a bachelor's degree. This group, representing approximately fifty-four million Americans, are potential students for companies focused on vocational training or degree pathway learning.

An additional sixty-two million high school graduates, age twenty-five or older in 2012, did not pursue any formal education beyond high school. Combined, this equated to over one hundred million prospective students for shorter-term vocational training or nontraditional degree level programs, areas of higher education touted by President Obama as an opportunity to improve America's competitiveness.

* * *

The prolific elimination of underperforming campuses and programs, in recent years, has positioned the career education sector for a return to growth and profitability without compromising its long and steady reputation as the leading vocational training provider at the postsecondary level. In this century, transparent operators offering high-quality, low-cost, regulatory compliant, relevant programs may rise to the top by leading the way in training the sixty-five percent of Americans that may never earn a bachelor's degree or higher.

And the degree-granting online career sector colleges and universities will need to differentiate to compete with the burgeoning nonprofit online players. Serving students rejected or failed by the traditional degree granters is noble indeed, yet more must be done to expand the cohort of students served.

That written, the entire sector's present struggles remain noteworthy. Regardless of programs offered or credentials conferred, an education company's intrinsic value toward becoming, or remaining, a great place to learn and earn for students and other principal stakeholders, will be measured by its willingness to put people first; build a campus or online platform of distinction; hire, train, monitor, and motivate passionate faculty, staff, and administrators; include relevant stakeholders in the major decision-making; follow a prescribed set of simple rules for everyday success, and forever play the game the right way.

David J. Waldron is a former campus president in postsecondary career education and the author of self-improvement books for those seeking to achieve the personal and professional goals that matter most in their life.

In addition to *A Great Place to Learn & Earn*, David has written three other nonfiction books. His latest effort, *Build Wealth with Common Stocks*, is a case study on his market-beating family portfolio. *Hire Train Monitor Motivate* offers practical career-building strategies toward improving organization, team, or individual career achievements in the hyper-competitive local and global marketplaces. *The Ten Domains of Effective Goal Setting* provides a workable template with a simple, holistic, and attainable objective toward a happier and more rewarding life, whether at home, school, play, or the workplace.

He is working with his wife, Suzan, on her memoir, *One of a Million Faces*, about living and coping with Type 1 diabetes and its complications.

David earned a Bachelor of Science in business studies as a Garden State Scholar at Stockton University and completed The Practice of Management Program at Brown University. He and Suzan reside in historic South Central Pennsylvania, USA.

Take control and achieve your dreams at davidjwaldron.com.